GET OFF
THE GRID!

ALSO BY SAUL GOODMAN

Don't Go to Jail! Saul Goodman's Guide to
Keeping the Cuffs Off

GET OFF THE GRID!

SAUL GOODMAN'S GUIDE TO STAYING OFF THE RADAR

Saul Goodman as Told to Steve Huff

A THOMAS DUNNE BOOK ≈ ST. MARTIN'S PRESS NEW YORK

THOMAS DUNNE BOOKS.

An imprint of St. Martin's Press.

GET OFF THE GRID! Copyright © 2017 by TM & © 2017 by Sony Pictures Television, Inc. All rights reserved. Printed in the United States of America. For information, address St. Martin's Press, 175 Fifth Avenue, New York, N.Y. 10010.

www.thomasdunnebooks.com

www.stmartins.com

Designed by Steven Seighman

The Library of Congress Cataloging-in-Publication Data is available upon request.

ISBN 978-1-250-07888-9 (hardcover)

ISBN 978-1-4668-9141-8 (e-book)

Our books may be purchased in bulk for promotional, educational, or business use. Please contact your local bookseller or the Macmillan Corporate and Premium Sales Department at 1-800-221-7945, extension 5442, or by e-mail at MacmillanSpecialMarkets@macmillan.com.

First Edition: April 2017

10 9 8 7 6 5 4 3 2 1

Contents

GET OFF THE GRID!

Introduction

Burn After Reading!

Hey, good to see you again! Saul Goodman, here—your captain of the Good Ship Reasonable Doubt, very happy to welcome you aboard for voyage numero dos! Perhaps you once knew me as Jimmy McGill (or maybe even "Slippin' Jimmy" if you met me before the spirit of the law swept me under her noble wing). Call me what you will, as long as it's not late for happy hour.

For the purposes of our chat today: names don't really matter—Saul, Jimmy, Flippity, Flappity. These days, there's a totally different name on my state-approved identification. That same jejune moniker adorns the rental agreement to my humble fifty-shades-of-beige, extended-value apartment—not to mention a number of other very important documents of record, including a birth certificate with conceivably accurate information. And while I mentally and spiritually remain a New Mexican bar-certified legal eagle . . . we're not quite there anymore, Toto.

Once upon the not-too-distant past, I got into a bit of a jam that led to a bit of a rabbit hole and long journey short, here we are—ready to rumble in the jungle of smoke screens and pseudonyms. For the purposes of discussion, however, it's just fine if for the duration of our conversation you still think of me as your old friend-at-law Saul.

Last we met, I detailed a variety of crazy wrinkles in the law that might bring clients to my office for a close encounter with *moi;* I then shared how I would give them my all and send them back into those refreshing (and scorching) Albuquerque rays of freedom. What you are reading now is a very different sort of legal guide, one that law enforcement officers might even consider *extra*legal. This is a unique map to aid those of you in need of getting the hell out of Dodge. Or Cicero. Or pretty much anywhere, if your fate du jour isn't treating you right and you need to make a drastic change, *tout suite.*

In this hyperconnected age, with everyone's pay stubs and grocery lists and double rainbow photos flying around the cyber world at the speed of a click, there's one thing that simply feels impossible to do: disappear. Sure, there are wild-eyed hermits in the Appalachian woods with Unabomber beards and big hearts who will tell you they've disconnected from the Matrix. They'll say they aren't just off the grid, they're actually invisible. And H.G. Wells, eat your heart out: they're probably correct . . . to some degree. There are men and women who have shed, shredded, and destroyed all connection to the hive mind.

Changing your 'do and floating off on your own like a balloon fleeing an absentminded kid's fingers toward a lonesome, deflated death in a tree is one way to disappear. Granted, not paying taxes for a while sounds great, but what if you're jonesing for a fresh start that can't be satisfied by a top-notch dye job from your local barber or barberess?

This is my guide to getting off the grid, but it's not just a wistful account of my own vanishing act. I'll tell you about folks from all walks of life who attempted the same, to varying degrees of success. There are many valid reasons to prefer the less bloody side of "fight or flight," and there are just as many ways to start flapping those wings to get airborne. I was Jimmy, then I became Saul, and now I'm another guy entirely. I've got a new job, a new "look"—and, perhaps most importantly, a new outlook.

I know what it's like to need to get gone. It was pretty great to be Saul, right up to the point when things were no longer "All good, man." And I know you're thinking that a good-looking, intellectual man-about-town like myself probably charmed my way into First Class on that Invisibility Flight, but I had to pay a figurative arm and a leg for my ticket. Probably my left kidney, too. Part of the fee went to the people who helped me remain completely anonymous. They don't know me; I've never heard of them. So I won't be naming names, here—you've only got the legal artist formerly known as Saul to contend with now.

And I'm here to help you figure out if, why, and how you might want to do what I did. Then again, it might not be your cup of tea. I'll put you through a little boot camp in covering your ass before your assets. I'll be your travel alarm clock waking you up with an ear-splitting "BEEP" to all those little details of disappearance you never even knew you had to worry about.

This is a guide to living life like a spy in the midst of polite society—except with no covert mission on which to hang your rakish black hat. You'll learn to put on the (legally) stylish thinking caps of both James Bond and whichever handsome English devil is playing him now. Fact is, it all comes down to that instinctual question asked by spies and soldiers and anyone who's ever found themselves in a scrape since we were facing down saber-toothed tigers with pointy sticks: *do I want to get out of this alive?*

Obviously, this is all purely for your entertainment. Of course you shouldn't attempt to run from the hungry, fear-smelling, trouble-monster that is your life. No way should *anyone* ever try to dodge creditors, tax collectors, or the police (and, in some cases, temperamental former amours). I'm still a sworn officer of the court on the inside, my friend, and therefore cannot *seriously* encourage you to do anything that is illegal in any way.

But if you're going to devise a back-up plan (a purely hypothetical one of course)—do it right. I hope you get inspired and run with it, build a happy little yurt on a remote farm and live your life goat herding safely away from the madding crowd. As long as you haven't committed any crimes worth prosecuting, it's perfectly legal for adults in these blessed United States to vanish whenever they wish. There's no legal gravity holding you down, keeping you punching time cards and voting for whomever's won the he said, she said city council majority this year.

Make no mistake: rebooting your life is a job in its own right. A life is a gargantuan canvas with a lot of cracks and corners to fill. Flipping one upside down and giving it a new coat of paint with a different name and a location far away from the one it knew requires invention. It takes sacrifice, and you're going to get tired eyes and sizable calluses along the way.

The time is now! Pull on those work mitts. Maybe layer some surgical-style rubber gloves underneath. Grab a long-sleeved shirt, too, because welding your life into an attractive new shape puts off a lot of invisible UV rays, and you don't want to be surprised by second-degree burns when you wake up the next morning. Plus, you don't want to leave too many skin cells behind if you can help it—think about all of that easily sampled DNA.

Okay. I see you're ready to hop aboard with your protective gear and bindle. Let's get this New You Show on the road.

Why Would Anyone Do This?

⚖️

Whatever it is, it's hit the fan and the stink's in circulation. Clock's struck midnight on your old life and it's time to go, pumpkin.

You might be a criminal: no judgment from the counselor, here. Maybe you were selling some fresh green ganja, some fine-ass Purple Urkel laced with Alice B. Toklas, and a deal went sour. Or—still in that malefactor vein—it could be that you're the brawn who tags along to ensure the deal works to your boss's advantage, and there was a tragic misunderstanding. People got hurt, and you need to run. From everyone.

Or maybe you're not a criminal! Perhaps you're falsely accused, or just good people with bad troubles. Fine. As bad luck could have it, there's a chance you're a victim. You've got a roommate with a head full of steam who doesn't appreciate when you forget to do the dishes, and you've noticed recently that the Gatorade in the fridge has been tasting a little antifreeze-y. Or you just discovered the nest of RGB cables in your bedroom's air-conditioning vent that feeds from cameras hidden in all crannies of your condo, and you're not looking to be one man's private reality show.

Next stop on the ominous train, maybe you're a lone survivor. You got a look at the devil's face and know he may come for you before the good guys (cops, in this case) ever even get close.

Any of these situations justly and naturally warrant a fresh start. The moment has come for you to strip off the heavy shell of you-ness and get a new beginning, a new name and a new life. It's time for a little karmic remodeling.

I will now state the obvious (for posterity): once you get to this point, you'd better know exactly why you bothered.

I, Saul, the man with the plan and the best friend you could have standing next to you before a no-nonsense New Mexico judge, didn't shoulder the burden of anonymity lightly. Not to give too much of the farm away (I'm going to act as if those acres of attorney-client privileges still apply, even if they don't), but I had life-preserving reasons for renovating my existence.

So let's lay down a little list of possible motivations any dear reader might have for following Mr. Low Profile's winding path to the sensibly khaki-clad life of an average civilian.

Legit Logic

There are plenty of reasons to walk (or sprint) away from an established "you," and although necessary, some of those reasons are unpleasant.

A disappearance at times begins as an "accident." You might recall some version of a news story that goes something like this: Miss Jane Doe ventured out for a drive on a winding mountain road on a cold winter's night. Alas, something—presumably fog and ice— prevented the lovely Miss Doe from arriving at her destination. Worst-case scenarios are often crafted by a sprinkle of pessimism and a dose of common sense. Customary earnest and hurried searches ensue, but Miss Doe has become a ghost of the mountain, at one with the mist in the pines.

Most likely, Miss Doe's car will be recovered from a

river a couple years later, her skeletal remains still sensibly seat-belted in place, phalanges yet clutching that "World's Greatest Auntie!" travel mug that never quite fit its holder. It's grim, but more commonplace than it should be. Bad things happen to good people, and there's not always someone in the forest to hear the sound of the tree falling. But as often as legitimate accidents occur, there are also plenty of "accidents" orchestrated by folks who are desperate to win the ultimate game of hide-and-seek.

No matter the circumstances, let's assume you need a brand-new bag. You, of your own volition, have chosen to make a change.

Getting off the grid is not for the half-hearted. Even the fully hearted might find this process intimidating. That's why it's normally—if such a thing is ever entirely normal—within the purview of feds and spies. If the government decides you're a pivotal witness in a federal case, you'll be masterfully transitioned right the hell out of your old life and into an untraceable new one. Intelligence services are the million-point "ASS" top score on the Centipede machine-style champs at this kind of thing.

Here's an example: a few years ago, a guy called Mahmoud was assassinated in a Dubai hotel. He was involved in some military operations far from the Israeli stamp of approval. Sure enough, the couple dozen suspects in Mahmoud's death were allegedly Israeli intelligence agents. They'd managed to acquire stolen British, Irish, German, French, and Aussie identification documents. The case remains unsolved because those intel agents (or whoever they were) vanished into the ether with their purloined passports.

There will be times here when it will feel like we're talking about spycraft; some of the behaviors required by this leaving-the-grid thing are fantastically furtive. Though you won't be assassinating anyone in Dubai. I hope.

To be crystal clear—and this is my inner counselor talking—this stuff isn't exactly all that legal, in the end. There may be gray areas, but generally it's safe to assume that the things we're discussing would not be recommended by our pals who live to protect and serve.

There's a big "but!" here. Dodging many of the obligations an intentional disappearance leaves behind may create a sticky wicket or two as far as the law's concerned, but that doesn't mean you shouldn't do it when and where the proverbial rubber meets the road.

Sometimes you've got to look out for numero uno. The following is a selection of motivations (appreciated but not necessarily endorsed by the former Saul Goodman) for jumping ship to the desert, the forest, or even the fine shores of the Missouri River:

- **Escaping violence.** Easily one of the strongest bases to light out for the provinces is the natural desire to get the hell away from some abusive buffoon. It's unnatural and unadvised to ignore pure survival instinct. While physical vengeance may seem more gratifying and perhaps simpler, it is by far the messier option. If anything here helps get someone out, out, and away from a sadistic prick, a savage clown, a nasty sociopath, a human skid mark, etc., I'll consider my mission accomplished.

- **Letting your wild passion decide.** When it comes to reasons for giving everyone who knows you the slip, escaping into the arms of your soul mate— über-bestie, side nugget, whatever the kids say now—is one of the most complicated of the bunch. You know the phrase "Hell hath no fury"? If you're reading up on ways to hightail it out of a marriage to get with the most desirable new stranger imaginable, just be aware that few are more motivated to find you and make you explain what you did than a jilted lover. It's not your fault that you've got such a magnetic personality! But think of the broken hearts that you're leaving in your wake as little paper clips: they're going to go chasing right after your attractive iron heart, and it won't be easy to repel them. So maybe save

yourself the hassle and—instead of disappearing—
go about ending things in a more straightforward
way if you can? Then grab your new sweetie and
move one town over—you probably won't get
burned by any old flames at your new local grocery store.

- **Dodging debts.** Although I think skipping out on
financial obligation is a semi-decent reason to
dissolve your current existence, it sets you up for
failure. There's a basic, inalienable desire among
creditors of all kinds—the legal and the illegal—
to hunt debtors down and make them pay. The
law circumscribes a plethora of above-board action that creditors can take these days, but that
hasn't quelled their Old Testament–style rage when
the amount owed is massive and the borrower is
missing. As we'll see, personal vanishing acts are
costly enough without collectors in pursuit.

With the legal kind of creditor, you may be
able to get away with a few basic adjustments:
changing your name, home address, and social
security number might do the trick. Unfortunately, lenders can leverage the courts to send the
law after you by filing suits that require you to
appear in court. Some state laws are more aggres-
sive than others. No show at court? A warrant

goes out, and *blammo!* You're wanted. That said—
they aren't high-priority warrants, unless you in-
curred a seriously huge debt and handled things
in a suspicious way. On the flip side, there are *illegal* debts, which are another subject entirely. That
leads me to . . .

- **Bad guys want to get you.** You've heard tell of federal witness protection. There's many a true-crime
miniseries about getting away from the tentacles
of the cartel or the mob or the mystery book of
the month club. Within all that drama and glam-
our is a rare but bare necessity. . . .

All too often, the tortoise-toed government
might not be in a rush to whisk you away from
that guy with a teardrop tattoo who's expressed
an uncontrollable desire to fry you up in a nice
butter sauce. You and the bureaucrats may not
feel the same sense of urgency about the matter.
Even if the feds are patrolling the block on your
behalf, there are simply times when the wolves
are way too close to the door and an extralegal
extraction must be performed. Those times cer-
tainly do include the collection of deadly debts
for drugs, for illegal services, for *legal* services.
Sometimes, you just know too much and there's a
guy who simply can't afford your existence any-

more. My friend, I support your existence. If you have to vanish because a wolf in human form is at the door with a cleaver and a smile, then get thee gone with my blessing.

Shaky Ground

I hate to be the guy to bring the comedown. It's not my thing to pass judgment. If it had been, I might have wound up on the other side of the big oak bench. I might have been a less successful attorney-at-law and a more successful judge-at-large. But as it stood, my clients didn't pay me to judge. Evaluate, sure. Counsel, yes. Level with them when necessary, if needed? Of course.

And yet . . . in the interest of covering as many bases as one man can (and I want to hit a homerun here!), even I have to admit that there are perfectly terrible reasons to disappear.

- **Dead-beating the rap.** In my legal practice, I was happy to be Albuquerque's very own inflatable Statue of Liberty. I'll take in those tired, poor, huddled masses. Even wretched refuse needs an attorney at some point. Still, I did sometimes get a little twinge of conscience if it seemed a client was trying to get out of paying for childcare or another dependent-related obligation. But still, it takes *funds* to pull this kind of thing off. My two cents is worth a lot more than advertised, and I'd like to offer that unless you have been breeding like a lecherous rabbit, the price of disappearing is going to be much greater than the price of child support.

- **Fraud gone bad.** Even in my unusual circumstances, I don't mind declaring that fraud is mostly unpropitious. Though, let's face it, some forms of fraud are slightly understandable. Hypothetically, let's say you laundered money for drug dealers and made it a habit to skim a bit. You're a modern-day Robin Hood, robbing from the rich and giving to the poor. The poor, in this case, being yourself. Who could blame you? One day, a contact seems more suspicious than usual. You get the feeling that it's time to take your stash and run, and more power to you.

  Or, perhaps you're "in the game," but you're not the type to play at the high-stakes table. There are low-yield frauds that take from the rich insurance companies and give to the poor slip-and-fall artists, though those situations rarely rise to the level of slipping out of life as you know it.

WHY WOULD ANYONE DO THIS?

Don't read me wrong—little seeds of fraud can grow into giant, uncontrollable beanstalks. I read about a guy—we'll just call him John Woe—who teamed with his wife in a doozy of a life insurance fraud. They took some clothes out of John's closet and played dress-up with a corpse they'd acquired, stowing John Woe's deceased doppelganger inside a soon-to-be-burned-out car. When ole Johnny came up "missing," Mrs. Woe received an impressive payday from her hubby's life insurance company. Unfortunately for the Woe-ful duo, the insurers tested the corpse's DNA and discovered the deception. As the icing on this morbid cake, the grieving Mrs. Woe promptly got a new boyfriend who was a not-so-dead ringer for her recently deceased husband, and the jig was up. Look, if you're going to try to fake your own death so that someone else can collect the insurance money, you've got to be okay with never, ever touching a penny of that sweet payout yourself. Your fake death only works if it operates on the same prevailing characteristic of your real death: it's permanent. So unless you were looking to get separated and you're feeling especially charitable toward your soon-to-be ex, don't try this one at home.

- **In a word, murder.** If sending a guy or gal a one-way ticket to Belize seems like the most direct solution to some very thorny problems, you'd better be geared up to weather the subsequent shitstorm. There was a Foreign Service officer in the '70s who had killer language skills and a boatload of degrees. A regular Man from U.N.C.L.E. Oh, and he offed his entire family with a hammer and then disappeared from the face of the earth. He had the skill set and the lead time on the cops to get the hell out of the United States and begin a new life elsewhere, speaking any one of the five dialects he knew as fluent as a native would. If you have a talented tongue and a ride out of town, by all means—you do you. But why not just disappear, and skip the gruesome part?

Now, my friend, is the time to grab another cup of coffee or your choice of energy concoction. We're getting off the stick. Like the old Morning Zoo Deejays used to scream, we're locking into this channel now and breaking the knob off.

Imagine that I'm about to upend a big old tub of Lincoln Logs and we're going to take a look at each one. By the time we're done, we'll have a built you a sturdy new life, your old self left behind. That shiny, newly named you will go striding off into the future.

Ha. No, seriously: best-case scenario is you get to the other side alive. You will be one lucky son of a gun or daughter of fortune if that wobbly toy house doesn't fall apart in the first breeze. But see, that's part of the fun—figuring out how we get to the end, so we can begin again.

A Plan, a Man, Something About Panama

Lawyering took an eye for details. I had to be able to spot a misplaced decimal on a shady accountant's spreadsheet the way a keen '49-er could see a fleck of gold in ten pounds of sand.

I can guarantee that if someone disappears, a focused acumen as sharp as mine will come knocking on your door. Thorough and patient peepers will absolutely find that one detail that you glossed over in your hurry to trip the light fantastic out of town before the villagers arrived with their torches.

Here's some tough love: you are going to forget something. Doesn't matter if you're an astrophysicist or actress—particulars necessary to getting off the grid will fly right through your nervous brain.

Let's start by ticking off a number of things that

might help anyone find you if you up and run tomorrow. I'm talking about seemingly everyday items you probably don't think too hard about as you glance at them in your wallet: credit cards, driver's license or state-issued ID, passport if you ever had one, and your good old social security number.

The short list of documents that validate your existence as a semi-functioning adult? They offer a formidable set of obstacles on the journey into a new life. Can't live with 'em, can't live without 'em. And if you're starting over? These papers are the tip of a digital iceberg of interconnected information. You definitely can't use them to set up your new life. You've got to start from scratch.

What You Leave Behind (Spoiler Alert: Everything!)

I'll assume by this point that you're totally clear on why you're doing this in the first place. That's settled business. Moving on to plan proper.

Feels kinda exciting, doesn't it? Woo-hoo! A new you! But before you dive into the deep end and start swimming to shores unknown, take a very hard look at the life you have right now, as you sit here. We've got to examine what we're leaving so we can understand how to get gone.

Those everyday marks, the hoi polloi in the streets drinking bubble tea and taking selfies with their dogs, don't realize they are happy little flies caught in a black widow's web.

Ever seen a black widow's web? The most deadly spider to ever ruin a rural trip to the outhouse makes this nasty-looking, haphazard death net in the most surreptitious nooks and crannies. None of that pretty *Charlotte's Web*–looking spiral art: just a cloud of silk. Lot of dead bugs wrapped up in there, though. Life's like that web, and whatever it is that has you ready to skedaddle is the black widow. And she's always hungry.

The only way to understand what you're doing is to take stock of all the threads that have you trapped in that predator's nest. That'll include our happy little list of flammable papers, like those pesky birth certificates.

And then: there are the digital threads. Go ahead. Park your name between a set of quotation marks in your favorite online search engine. Unless you've got a common name like "Bill Smith" or "Jane Jones," chances are any number of the results kicked back to you will, in fact, be you. If you have social media, like Facebook or Twitter or Twitface—whatever—there are friend and family connections weaving you tighter into the Web. Your quotidian interactions with these folks leave behind a bread-crumb trail to be gobbled up by the powers-that-be.

Already getting the picture, I hope. To truly separate from that old life, you are going to have to get out your proverbial machete and chop right through that jungle of connections. More of them spring up to block your path every day! It's not going to be easy, but you've got to face up to just how many cords need to be cut.

If you have additional licenses—law, business, marriage, guns, weed, scuba, etc.—those are all sets of silken threads vibrating under that imaginary spider's feet.

Records for all these things are often readily searchable. It's a lead-pipe cinch to look up a business license in a state database. A committed investigator with any agency—private or public—can study those records and suss out all sorts of salient details, like what your actual signature looks like. That's in there if you signed the documents the kindly clerks at the state business registry thingy saw fit to turn into easily downloadable PDF documents. And hey, what about that marriage license? Or licenses? That's a document and even better (or worse, for our purposes), another person who has plenty of information they might be willing to part with should one of the reasons you're seeking a new name and life come a-knocking at their door.

Then there's family. This is a crazy wrinkle, because if you are without blood relations, well hey, perhaps that's a choice and good for you. If that's the case, your situation would make our job here easier, because when you're trying to escape an old life for a new, family ties may be some of the toughest to untangle.

Most folks have a tendency to talk to family with reckless abandon. You go away suddenly one day with no notice to Mom or Pop or even your brother, one of them might remember the time you openly fantasized about doing just that—leaving this crapfest rat race of a life behind with dreams of glory.

Getting off the grid requires you to be on your guard, all the time. Don't get too comfortable. You've got to stay three steps ahead. Before you can even consider cutting loose and stepping off, you have to know where you're escaping to. You've got to go set up your new home, in whatever form that may take.

Before I grab my hammer and start whacking the brass tacks of your new digs into place for you, it's only fair I impart some of my own experience, give you some idea of how it works if you decide to involve another freelance contractor in this hootenanny. I'll be really real with you: it's sticky, spooky, and 'spensive . . . but an intermediary can help guide you on the yellow brick road to your very own Oz.

The Basics

Let's say you're in a tough position. You've gotten your-self into a tangle with some unsavory characters work-ing on a dangerous project, and man, can you ever see the electrified piss lightning bolts on the horizon. You don't have to be psychic to know how many things are falling apart. So what's to do?

The solution is to get away, to get anywhere. Maybe you could find a job working fast food at a mall in a snowy Midwestern city—because who the hell would think to look for a fugitive there, right?

Maybe in this situation you simply don't have time to sit down with a book like this, or noodle around on the Dark Web. Remember when you were in high school and you had the sneaking suspicion that all the cool kids were hanging out and brewing moonshine without you? Well, if they weren't then—they are now, virtually and anonymously on the shady digital alleys of the Dark Web. Prepubescent moonshine is probably the tamest thing you could acquire there.

WHY WOULD ANYONE DO THIS?

If you don't have time to wander the maze-like cess-
pool of the secret Internet to find an escape hatch from
your life: that's when you will probably want to start
hunting for someone local who already has his or her own
nefarious sources and some practice providing others
with vetted, authentic papers that the happy folks at
border patrol wouldn't blink twice at if you wanted to go
on a little jaunt to Canada to stock up on maple syrup or
maple whiskey or maple lima beans, whatever it is you're
in the mood to eat.

We can call these friendly and helpful merchants
"identity brokers," though that's a confusing term because
it might also refer to the scum of the earth services that
harvest the e-mail address from your "Coffee Cake Digest" subscriptions and shop it around to a million other
mailing lists that you're probably not interested in (unless
you like your spam with a side of "GROW TEN
INCHES IN TEN HOURS TO PLEASE YOUR
MAN!")—sometimes those services are called identity
brokers, too.

Our brand of identity brokers are a little bit like
drug dealers, except instead of hallucinogenic lollipops,
they're doling out passports and IDs. They frequently
do their work for nice people born out of town who seek
to grab that brass ring of American citizenship. Co-
lombians anxious to try Seattle's Best Coffee, Russians

looking to ditch the fur boots for a pair of white Nikes, English folks who discover they're Anglophobes—the usual suspects. Here's how that might play out . . .

Let's say our neighborhood ID retailer is Sam. If you don't know who your neighborhood ID retailer is, just nonchalantly wander under the bleachers at your local high school and ask the chain-smoking, fifteen-year-old sipping from a bottle wrapped in a brown paper sack. She'll tell you who has the goods, for a price.

Sam learns that Ricardo in Mexico City is seeking to shed the skin of his old life in the *ciudad* and start anew in Albuquerque. New Mexico sounds like just the place to be his new Mexico! Sam has a connection in Puerto Rico—which is a U.S. territory, for those of you who missed that day in your elementary school geography class—and his guy in San Juan has amassed a tasty collection of vital papers. We're talking social security cards, birth certificates, and other personal docs donated willingly (or more likely, without the consent of) by-God true American citizens. Puerto Rico ships off this solid info from people who may not even know it's been stolen or are too dead to care, and then our fine businessman Sam hands over a matching set of social security card and birth certificate to Ricardo for a cool $2,000.

Ricardo gets ready to live in the land of enchantment and Sam lines his pockets with some sweet, sweet pesos.

That's a simple breakdown of how one guy could change his identification and gets away with it, but let's be real: he's walking above a pit of tigers on a tightrope made of dental floss. Even if there is no evidence the vital info is stolen and no computer alarms go off, Immigration and Customs agents are on this kind of scheme like guac on corn chips. There's a non-trivial chance that this set-up is a self-writing headline about the ICE busting up a Puerto Rican pipeline of immigration fraud.

The takeaway here is that the procedure for securing a new ID in-country, through a different broker and without the pesky problem of having to finagle a passport, is a little safer than trying to provide Ricardo from Mexico City with his new start as Diego from San Juan, a legally papered U.S. citizen. Yeah, it's the whole border-crossing thing that gets you.

Unless you're a bird, salmon, or tarantula: adding the immigration element makes travel much more difficult. So let's set that aside and just deal with brokering a new identity that keeps you inside your national borders.

To cut a long story short and save us both the headache and future court appearance: this method? It's not worth it.

"But Saul," you wail in distress, "you—you—you

hypocrite!" Yes, I know. I had a guy who knew a guy and all that, and hey, *voila*, here we are: me in this shadowy place with a new life and you frustrated I just told you my solution might not work for you.

Just remember that as a state-sanctioned officer of the court, it was often my pleasure to defend what our judgmental society might call "the dregs." Folks who were in dire need of creative and charismatic representation in the courtroom.

Plenty of my clients paid in cold, hard cash. A few, though, had to make arrangements. If you're the type of guy who collects friends easily, maybe you should consider making the acquaintance of a few less-than-savory characters (all of whom have hearts of gold, their mothers will swear!) who might be able to hook you up when the turkey hits the tarmac.

If you're not blessed with such a varied social circle, what you'd have to do in order to find a contractor willing to do all this scut work might not be practical. The corners of the Internet where mysterious identity brokers ply their trade are also full of nasty crap like the types of porn that are illegal in all nations and would likely make the devil himself turn up his nose. Sure, you could find marketplaces for authentic new passports and driver's licenses—but the danger factor is way too high.

I've guided clients through some treacherous waters before, but I can't look over your shoulder and say "don't click that" or "not sure it's a good idea to call that number." Just imagine: you could be shaking some fresh ground pepper all over your Caesar salad while you browse the Dark Net and then—*achoo!*—your index finger slips and two weeks later, your youthful new bride Oksana is ringing the doorbell. Whoops! So that's my word on getting a broker to ferry you across the river into your new life: the risk may not be worth the reward for the future Miss Ann Onymous.

What to Do Before You Do It

So now that we've kicked the tires on that "buy your way to a new you" idea and sent it rolling off into the ocean: back to our regularly scheduled programming.

Becoming a person with a different life is a thing people generally only dream about. I'm not talking to the dreamer now, I'm all about the doer. At this point, a doer has a ballpark idea of when he or she wants to pull the trigger and go POOF from the orbits of old friends, family, and kind-hearted creditors.

For some, circumstances may dictate that date. I know for me, it was pretty clear when it was time to go.

I looked around and saw that the last chopper out of Saigon had a seat with my name on it.

Of course I had help, but hey, you don't pass the bar without being a stellar self-starter. I learned a lot from the good folks who assisted me, and I'm passing these savings on to you.

First thing's first: planting the seeds of that new life as far in advance of your exit date as possible. Let's break down what you might have to do. . . .

A New Name!

So what do you want to be called? If you have some terrible burden of a name like Eldon P. Squatcobbler or Bertha Burgerboffer, there might be a temptation to go for something much cooler, like Heather Supermodel or James M. McGill. Cue the descending slide whistle on that sort of ego stroking, friend—that's the worst approach. Bland, bland, bland. The watch word is "bland." Manila envelope bland. Suburban strip mall stationery store bland, *capisce?*

Okay, once you've selected an appropriately milquetoast nom de plume, it's time to consider options for legally acquiring that name.

That's an option, you know: quietly and covertly changing your name in court. Having said that, the law is arranged to weed out name-change requests done to avoid debt, angry spouses, or Colombian neckties paid for by some cartel boss with a winter home in Tijuana and a Rottweiler named "Pequeño." A legal name change still leaves a paper trail that stands out like dandruff under a blacklight. And it's not just unprofessional, it's potentially fatal. Everything is potentially fatal, I agree, but this is *painful* fatal.

So, jumping back into the hypothetical end of the pool . . . let's just skip the legal means and get right into the splashy fun part: identity theft!

Are You Down with O.P.P.I. (Other People's Personal Information)?

The good folks who assisted me in transferring to the glamorous Undisclosed Location Lifestyle I currently lead let me in on this surprising secret: you can steal someone else's identity just about as easily as you could pluck a candy bar from a baby's greasy fingers. To paraphrase celebrity exponent of the Boston accent Matt Damon in the film adaptation of *The Talented Mr. Ripley*, it's almost easier "to be a fake somebody than a real no-body."

Identity theft is frequently used just to gain access to the victim's money, but we're higher minded than that, aren't we? Forget about that other guy's money, we just need this new name to make it easier to fade into the woodwork! That's the thing about an existing ID: it may not be what you stick with, but it can help you acquire the documents you need to, say, fool Canadian border patrol just enough to make it across before you disappear under yet another moniker into those majestic lowlands.

How Do I Steal Someone's Identity?

Whoa, there! Listen, I can't tell you how to do something illegal like that! I can, however, give you some idea of what I've learned other people may have tried. This is purely for educational purposes, obviously.

It's not the kind of thing we think about every day. If it were, it would probably leave us paralyzed with paranoia. But here's the big, spooky secret behind identity theft: it's really easy for anyone who knows what they're doing, because information about us is *everywhere*. Your bank statements (sent by mail or digitally), utility bills, your subscriptions to both *Soap Opera Digest* and *Soap Opera Weekly* . . . we're social creatures and we need to have heat and electricity and a place to park our money, and we don't always realize just how vulnerable that makes us.

So say you're a forty-something male of medium height—or a thirty-something woman who's taller than average, whatever works—and you are about the right weight for your age, have thinning or dyed hair, brown eyes, clubbed toes, third nipples. Seek first that which you see in the mirror. As in, someone who kind of reminds you of yourself. That's what an identity thief might do, anyway.

Now that you've acquired your mark, it's time to do some research.

Here's a select list of some of the ways an enterprising identity thief might go about boning up on their target:

- **Getting the mail!** Only it's another person's mail, not yours. Just about any piece of mail can provide nuggets of information for you to use. Christmas cards from Grandma give you family information and names, credit card bills can clue you into a person's financial stability (like, if the bill is three months behind, maybe don't steal this poor sap's identity; that'd just be cruel), as well as provide you with account numbers.

- **Pickpocketing.** I'm not trying to send a ragtag crew of readers out into the cold like some creepy Dickens character leading a pack of orphaned thieves. A really simple route to gathering almost all the info you need on someone whose identity you want to co-opt—just temporarily, and not for larcenous purposes, mind you—might be stealing their wallet. Go figure. Grab whatever you can, like social security cards and identification, then leave it someplace nearby so the unfortunate mark can maybe recover their Diners Club Card.

- **Internet.** The Internet is a monstrously great way to ferret out every tiny tidbit no one ever wanted you to know about them. There's data stored in bases online people don't even think about. Like that time you put your e-mail address up on a Deep Purple message board because you couldn't figure out the right chords to "Smoke on the Water." There are sites with old newspaper clippings that you can search and unearth the most mundane details about your mark, if they or their families were on the grid enough to show up in the local *Lunenburg Ledger* every now and then.

- **Dumpster diving.** How do private detectives do it? Cops? Fun fact: **garbage is in the public domain.** If the average Jane, Joe, Jim, or Juan was more paranoid, they'd realize that the crap they drop in the waste basket could give an ambitious identity thief a leg up on becoming, well, *them.* Yes, if you're the kind of guy or gal who habitually carries hand-sanitizing gel, this endeavor might be a nightmare for you, but sometimes you've just got to get down and dirty in pursuit of your mission.

Take it from someone who's gone fly fishing in the most pungent garbage you can imagine: dumpster diving is an athletic endeavor. I recommend that if you go this route, you know exactly what you're after and have a reasonable amount of confidence you will find it. Wear the crappiest clothes you own, rubber gloves, a mask to breathe through, and maybe down a solid belt of Old Grand-Dad before you hop into that big green box. Also—and this is the trick—your search and rescue mission should not be a daytime activity. Be armed with a flashlight and make your leap in the middle of the night.

Let me illustrate what I'm talking about with a little story . . .

Steve Snowman decided he wanted to become a guy he knew named Brian Bowman, who happened to be about the same age and have a similar hairline to Steve's. So: Steve plugged Brian's known info into a search engine of his choosing. Soon he knew where Brian was born, that he had an Akita named Evita when he was a kid, and that he claims to be the Internet's foremost authority on bespoke galoshes.

With these unsettling facts in hand, Steve drove to Brian's place and waited till his target dropped an innocuous black trash bag in the dumpster. Soon, Steve made off with the goods! Once he got home, he put a big cartoon clothespin on his nose and began peeling scribbled notes, bills, printed e-mails and out-of-date coupons from the mess. From his research, Steve then had a great idea as to what Brian's signature looked like, both printed and in old-fashioned script. He began practicing said signature right away. Not long after, Brian Bowman II could be found sailing around Bermuda in a boat named *Aweigh it Again, Sam.*

Moral of the story? Concentrate on the fundamentals for this stage of the festivities—social security numbers, ID, deep-cut information, family tree information that fleshes out your new false face.

Plant That Green

In my previous incarnation as a magically gifted and fashionably dressed Albuquerque attorney, I have to confess: I knew how to get that green. I won't say I was rolling in it, that wouldn't be modest. I did have my exit plan pretty firmly in place when I lit out for my new life, and that exit plan required *moolah*.

On the most fundamental level: if you don't have money, what are you going to do in your new life, anyway? Unless you plan on roughing it—more or less being homeless, which in this context still requires that you buy at least some basics like a backpack—mo' money means mo' choices. However, if you're a man or woman of limited means who is not wanted in seventeen states for crimes against nature or humanity, the good thing about disappearing for you may be the same thing that makes unfortunate disappearances of the poor so sad— the state just won't work that hard to try and find you again.

I don't know what your time line is, but start socking away the exit funds now. For everything we're about to muddle through together, money is your best friend . . .

. . . Unless the dear reader is Bill Gates–level rich, that is. If you're so wealthy that the massive pot you have to piss in is made from fourteen karat gold, why are you even reading this? Because while you've got the means to blow town at a moment's notice, all those Franklins crowding your bank account mean you have a much larger target on your back.

What I'm getting at is: the best candidate for using anything from our pleasant chat here to move on up to a deluxe apartment under another name and credit rating is probably some middle-of-the-road schmoe with just enough disposable income to start putting a sizable chunk away each month.

Squirreling the Green Away

It's not fair to beat this money drum and not give you a few ideas as to how to become a cadet in the marching band. Here are a few suggestions as to how to jump into your new skin with a little bit of cash in your pocket. The best part is: many are 100 percent legal. Mostly.

Work it. If you are willing to forego a good night's sleep, get a second job. Or a first one, or a third one—

depending on how many you had already. This is no time to act high and mighty: take stock of the kind of grunt work you can handle, and get to grunting. Whatever you choose to do—be it mowing lawns, loading trucks, or spinning signs outside a realty company—put as much of every little check away as you can. Though, if the local strip club wants to cover your car with some scantily clad skin for a cool $5,000 a month, that kind of mobile-billboard advertising might draw more attention than the check is worth. Try not to take on a job so out-of-character that it might make folks around you suspicious.

Cash back! At many grocery and department store checkouts, we get the option when using debit-credit card machines to be handed some cash back. Every time you shop, add twenty bucks or a solid Benjamin to the bill and then tuck that cash away in an old Florsheim shoebox hidden deep in your closet. It might take some time, but eventually you'll be pretty impressed by the size of the nest egg you've built.

You can't take it with you. eBay, Craigslist, flea markets, whatever—start selling off everything you can think of. You probably won't need that state-of-the-art speaker system on the other side. Pare your life down to the bare minimum of comforts—it might be unpleasant in the present, but it means you'll have the capital to afford more of those luxuries when you get where you're going. So good-bye, collection of vintage *Tiger Beats*! That mint-condition pinup of Paul Revere and the Raiders has got to ship out to a happy home somewhere far away . . . and soon you will, too.

Ride shares, etc. Robert De Niro. Mel Gibson. James Cagney. You know what these three actors have in common, other than lustrous hair genes? They all portrayed characters who specialized in the exciting field of taxicab driving. This is similar to the "second job" option—but it's a lot more flexible these days. You'll get to meet new folks, have them barf in your backseat, and see the world you already know and are ready to get the hell away from. If you need that green, buddy—hoist up your rickshaw of choice and get moving!

These are just a few of the available options for setting up your get-away funds. And once you've collected your personal reserve? Never, ever, under any circumstance do a damned thing with it. No investments. No paper trail. Why? The IRS. Let's think about the fine men and women tasked with making sure we pay them the appropriate amount of blood money to keep the engines of the national machine cranking along— they're the most indefatigable bunch of debt collectors on the face of the planet. You think the police, the mob, the courts know best how to deal with those that have done them wrong? Just remember: *The IRS finally put Al freaking Capone away.*

If a Public Enemy No. 1 like Capone couldn't escape the long ledger of the Internal Revenue Service, don't expect that you can, either. In all these things we're talking about, the most important thing to avoid at every turn is playing Hansel and Gretel with anyone who might one day be moved to come through the forest chasing after you with a big old axe.

Paper, Paper Everywhere, and No Sign of Me

I don't want anyone who reads these words to ever get arrested and put away for a painfully long time in a federal penitentiary with access only to monochromatic closed-circuit television. We're just spitballing here, right?

So, continuing with our purely academic discussion, here goes: this is how you could theoretically obtain some of the crucial fake or otherwise sketchy papers you'll need to morph into your newest self . . .

Not for the Faint of Heart

There are a ridiculous number of ways to get fake papers, but none of them are that easy, all are prone to fatal flaws, and—in the interest of brutal honesty—it's getting harder to obtain them every day. In other words: the food is terrible, and in such small portions!

You and I, we're mere mortals. We're at the mercy of a lot of powerful machines. Stuff that can't be fooled by a little white-out and a winning smile. I'm talking about the biggest stumbling block when it comes to crafting fake documents: even if you create one that's utterly convincing, featuring all the requisite materials (the cleverly hidden little hologram of an eagle, scannable bar code, and "I Heart America!" watermark), it could still go bust if databases trade your info fast enough to come up with a hit that indicates a problem. The bad fake doc problem will screw the unwary at borders and in airports nearly every time. Your best bet is to restrict yourself at first to a fake state-issued license or ID.

There are few ways to make it over the speed bump of acquiring one with your vehicle's suspension intact. . . .

State-Issued ID. This doesn't permit you to do anything but buy booze and cash checks. Well, it will also get you on most domestic flights. It's a dirt simple piece of identification to acquire—though in most states it helps if you have a birth certificate, proof of local address, and a past ID of some sort.

Let's say you've acquired the birth certificate. After that, the forgery part of the festivities isn't too complicated and at an average DMV it won't be scrutinized that closely. It won't be hard to draw up a fake electric bill to verify your identity, and the old ID needed could conceivably be altered from one of your own.

I'm over-simplifying, but let's consider the problem with a simple state ID in most places: no driving. Seriously, you may cruise not one mile per hour above the speed limit, but—there's still that outside chance you might run into an old-fashioned roadblock one night. Sober or not, your state identification isn't an operator's license—and everything would start to unravel then.

Of course there's another option, but it takes some finesse: straight up bribing a DMV employee to make a new driver's license for you.

First you've gotta suss out the most easily compromised DMV clerk. Sure, sure, the standard take on DMV drones is that they are deeply dissatisfied public servants who delight in torturing us with their control over our ability to freely move from strip mall to strip club. And while that's often the case, there are a few ripe peaches in that bushel who haven't turned rotten yet! However, that doesn't mean it's as simple as grabbing a big hunk of that cash you've been setting aside to lubricate said civil servant into handing you a totally authentic piece of fake identification.

To begin, take a few trips to the bureau of motor vehicles. Pick up various pamphlets from all corners of the room—or pretend you're waiting for an appointment, but you're too impatient to sit long. Stake the whole place out, get a feel for who's who. Eventually, you'll spot the easiest mark—surlier than average, perfunctory in every transaction, more monotonous than a white noise generator—and that's the clerk to keep an eye on. Even civil servants have needs! Figure out how to get some I-scratch-you-scratch action, and hopefully your new pal will be able to hook you up.

That's a very iffy plan, unless you go into it with a solid lead on a slippery employee. Let's sketch out how you might just take care of this issue yourself. . . .

Unleash your inner da Vinci! Admittedly that's not an artful way to put this, but I'm making a point: you may have to call upon all your considerable visual genius to enact this part of the plan.

Forging an identity card isn't that tricky, but be wary—many now come with a special bar code on the back that's encoded with your information. That bar code can tell anyone who laser scans it with the right software a ton of stuff about you.

For example: the bar code on the back of the Illinois state-issued license and nondriving ID contains only basic info like your name, its expiration date, and a couple of other bits of data. On a fake ID, I'd suggest this bar code needs to be half-plausible and programmed with something, but as long as you steer clear of airport security and drugstores that sell pseudoephedrine, it's likely no one will ask to scan your ID.

Ignore Web sites that offer fake IDs: they're mostly just after a quick buck, even on the so-called Dark Web. To make a temporary fake ID yourself, you will need a pretty up-to-date computer and a killer scanner. Use a little bit of the cash you've set aside to buy whichever one you need.

Start with an existing piece of identification that's essentially what you're looking to build. For example, if you're in Kentucky and are a six-foot tall white guy in your forties, politely borrow an ID from another dude who fits those specs. Then scan that puppy at the highest possible resolution.

Now pop that scanned image into your favorite image manipulation program and go to town. Steal the background color in the other guy's photo, then grab a photo of yourself and cut and paste it in there. Change whatever else you can think of to better build this identity in your own image.

Once all that artistic image manipulation is complete, examine your masterpiece closely. If it's satisfactory, you have another challenge to face: choosing the best stock on which to print.

Brothers and sisters, I know it's tiresome. These little picayune details are just killing you, right? But what price for a new life, friends? What's it worth to you to breathe that fresh air of freedom under a new name with that nasty old slate of yours newly wiped clean? You sat down and started reading, so here it is: we have to escape the devil at our heels by focusing on these details.

ID cards are printed on plastic or on paper that's coated (or specially laminated). It's important that you get as close as you can to what the state you're in really uses. Before you even begin the labor of cutting and pasting your handsome mug onto John or Jane Doe's ID scan, be sure you are clear on the kind of medium you'll be printing it on, be it PVC (polyvinyl chloride), Teslin, or whatever magical synthetic substance the federal government decides to make use of next.

So what if you're in New York and your fake license says it was printed in 2006? Order yourself up a stiff drink and a flimsy, bendable ID, because the tactile is just as important as the visual when it comes to fooling your local bar bouncers and bank tellers. Final touches will include sizing the card so it looks and feels right in the hands of whomever handles it, but if you've nailed the finer details, that's just busy work.

The Spookiest Option

Earlier, I said one of your options for fake identification was among the spookiest you could try. This is *the* spookiest, for several reasons. Those reasons include the fact it's one that's been used by spies—aka "spooks"—and it involves the dead.

That's right, we're talking about robbing the dearly departed folks who have barely begun to cool on a slab in the morgue.

Here is one tried-and-true method for copping another's name . . .

Obituaries. Keep a close eye on the death notices. If you are an African American male age forty-two, pay attention to blurbs about the demise of other black men who have just crested over the hill before fatally crashing into a telephone pole. Same if you're a Caucasian woman, age sixty-two—look for white ladies who had a little too much fun in their early retirement. You get the picture. Bank on a death in the biggest city close to you as well. Everyone knows everyone in a small town— you don't want to mistakenly acquire the identity of the Billy Joel of Podunk, USA.

Once you have a good match, pay close attention to how they went: if it was a particularly gruesome or violent death, that's not your target. Law enforcement and national news reporters alike will be flying circles above that body like investigative vultures. We're only interested in the unfortunate folks who passed relatively gently, from a rough go of pneumonia or a sudden cardiac event.

If you've happened on a decent candidate, track down his or her address. Here's where the endeavor gets extremely squirmy, so steel yourself and get thee to an improv class—you can either A: go to the decedent's (dead guy or gal's) house and pretend you are a long-lost friend from elementary school who happened to be glancing through the grisly pages. Once there, you might ask for a better photo to remember them by than the one on your prayer card. Or B: you can straight-out burglarize the place of vital documents. Nothing else, of course— we're not talking common criminality here, just some papers, that's all. What's the decedent going to need with those now?

At bare minimum, this will get you the foundation for securing some kind of *temporary* identification. There's a period after a recent death, and that period varies widely, when the deceased person's information is in limbo.

How that might work: much of the time, funeral directors are the folks who take vital information from death certificates or family records and bite the bullet of getting that stuff turned in to the authorities. Under their auspices, the dead person's social security number, for example, is reported to the very cheerfully named Social Security Death Index. Yes, as advertised, it's a big list of dead peoples' social security numbers.

There's no way that list is complete at any given time, but a good many of these folks who help burn up and bury our dearly departed are very serious about their jobs. It isn't, after all, a career path for the lighthearted. So the method for securing papers from the dead just outlined above has to either be for an identification intended for short-term use or—if you are really enterprising, not to mention plain good at stealing—you can chance snatching up the decedent's info before the funeral home gets hold of it. Fortune favors the bold!

CSI Your Life

Let's say you've established a solid new set of vital documents. On paper, the new you is well-established. Now all that's needed is to walk away from everything, right? Just put the necessities in a go-bag, drizzle some hi-test rum throughout the place, drop a match and walk. In the morning, the arson investigators will conclude you were roasted to a crisp. Hopefully this is something you do in your own discrete living space, not a shared condominium complex. I'll keep a happy thought, and assume that any fires lit will be contained only to the space you settled in alone, preferably surrounded by a hydrated moat or not-so-flammable dirt lot.

Truth is, before you make that final leap into the great and anonymous unknown, you have to think about those investigators in your burned-out life, and consider what they might be looking for.

The creation of a new life while still living the one you want to exit just leaves a trail. There will be digital evidence, physical evidence, even eyewitness evidence.

Ever see a cowboy movie where the hero is trying to evade the posse of bad guys and so he breaks off a tree branch and sweeps it along the path behind him, erasing his footprints? That's what we're doing here.

Damage Control

Resign yourself to the truth now, *compadre:* you left something behind. The best we can do is try and minimize the danger that presents to your future endeavors.

Computers are not your friend. Of course, they *are*—while you're cobbling together faked and altered papers, ordering necessary supplies, sending anonymous money orders, watching pornography, et cetera. Then, when it's time to light out, that shiny glass and metal rectangle that gently warmed your lap through many a nervous night has the potential to be your worst enemy.

If you leave your beloved electronic devices behind—any of them—you risk leaving an open invitation to dig into whatever digital trails you've established since you first purchased those machines.

Of course, if there's a relative lack of drama in your vanishing, then backtracking you through cyberspace won't be too appealing to investigating authorities. However, it's probably not the best idea to bank on the apathy of former friends, colleagues, and loved ones— even if they didn't always display interest or shower you with compliments, their curiosity might inspire them to do a little snooping into your digital underwear drawer.

So be thorough: clear your history and wipe that hard drive. But don't stop there!

As you prep to go, trash that laptop. You'll need to purchase something called a neodymium magnet. It's the most powerful magnet you can buy. Run that piece of electro-magic all over your laptop.

Then, take said laptop into the backyard (or any relatively private location) and with a handheld implement such as a sledgehammer, axe, or even a very large rock, proceed to beat the living daylights out of it. Then burn it. Throw the ashes into the ocean and call it a day.

I know this is all a bit much, but hey: I'm making a point here. It's just wise to eliminate those inroads into your life.

Proceed to do that with every digital thing you own. Phones, pagers, tablets, theremins: the works. For the love of all that was good and preprogrammable, take any copy machine you've ever touched and destroy it twice. Those things have a longer memory than the elephant you forgot to invite to prom.

It all sounds like a brutal waste of money, I admit, but this is where another preparatory measure might come into play: if you've laid aside that stash we talked about earlier, then the moment you're heading down the highway into new life city, you can hit up the next big box store you see and get some brand-new stuff. However . . .

About the Internet. This part is going to be tough. It might even be a deal breaker for some. We love the Internet, don't we? It's the most fun a thoroughly modern member of Western society can have by themselves . . . or with a group of faceless strangers.

But, now? You've got to cut ties, burn bridges. Do you frequently leave encouraging comments on You-Tube videos of make-up artists turning themselves into animals? Never watch another Beauty Vlog again—it's not worth the temptation to reveal yourself to a familiar community.

You might think the most surefire way to avoid playing Peeping Tom on your old life is simply obliterating all your accounts, but that type of mass deletion will send up red flags to those around you (not to mention the authorities). Don't do that! Simply stop using them. Never, under any circumstances, sign back in to nostalgically reread old messages from lovers, friends, and creditors. The moment you're done, you are <u>done</u>.

Which brings me to another crazy thing, a normal part of human nature. If you start a brave new digital presence with your recently acquired persona, here is the cardinal rule: never, ever become digital "friends" with anyone you ever interacted with on the Internet, if you can avoid it.

Think about the real world. Say every time in your

old life when you headed over to the King Soopers to grab an Italian sub from Jeff in the deli section, you guys shot the shit about how the Cubs were doing this season. Which, being the Cubs, was probably always bad—but it gave you and Jeff something to jaw about. In daily life, plenty of people have casual little connections like that, and we have a megaton of similar connections online.

Once you've left the old life of Timmy McNeal for the new life of, say, Paul Woodman, does it make a lick of sense to say, "Man, I'd love me an Italian sub from that King Soopers. I'll just say hi to Jeff while I'm there, see if he thinks we'll ever draft another Sammy Sosa."

No, it does not make sense. Same thing online, maybe even double. If you had a Twitter account and flirted with Ernesto from Santa Monica every day, it's an epic act of dipshittery to log on as totally new human being Alice Edmunds and start back up dreaming of life with old Ernie.

The bottom line is: separation. It's human to want to maintain connections, but we don't usually take stock of just how many of those we have. And herein is the huge challenge in going off that grid and laying low under an assumed name in a new city—truly letting go of everything you had before.

It can be done. It's an act of sheer will, sure, but look

at what you're doing: beginning a new life with a new name. You are, in essence, a baby.

Do babies come into this world with a network of friends and acquaintances outside Mom, Dad, and the odd sibling or two? Not really. Even the medical personnel who assisted in dragging us into this tornado of action forgot our names within a day of our birth. So open your crying maw and blink up at the sun, baby bird— your bright future awaits! But first . . .

Offline evidence. This here is simple housekeeping: clean up your crap. Let's say you went with a plan to alter an ID to suit your purposes. That leaves traces, including incriminating records in your printer's memory. Clean up all the evidence from that and deep-six it in a dumpster across town. Then smash that sophisticated printer. Make like the guys in *Office Space*. Treat it like you're Whitey Bulger getting rid of a snitch. Club that sucker into submission and set it on fire.

At the same time: you've got to act like a Girl Scout in a national park and leave no trace of yourself behind. Not even a footprint, if possible. Not everyone will have the means to pay a guy found by another guy to assist in the project, so in the process you've got to become your own guy. Or gal. Or whatever works for you, as long as you get gone.

Before we move on, I think it's a good time to offer a

little reassurance. You can do this, if your heart is really in it. Fact is, there are some folks who have done it and to this day we're not sure what happened to them. One guy, a poet, may have died the day he vanished, or he may have lived out his life in awesome anonymity. A dead body discovered on an Australian beach is a complete mystery today—that dude was very good at making sure no one knew who he was.

Then there's the German student who decided he liked America enough to stay, so he took English elocution lessons from *Gilligan's Island*. He ended up married to a millionaire and mistaken for a harmless New England eccentric before he screwed it all up.

And also ol' Joe, who may have been the best at this game—though he admittedly exited his first life before the advent of super computers and massive databases linked across states and nations. Nobody knows who Joe was to this day, and in his story you'll learn a thing or two about making your own departure, because Joe was a detail man till the very end.

PART II

Case in Point

Some lawyers love case studies. Me? Eh, sometimes. If the study isn't relevant to the case, it's good stuffing for the pillow you nap on in the corner of the law library.

When it comes to the subject of people who apparently/nearly succeeded at assuming new lives (until they did something stupid), case studies get interesting. At minimum, they're good for a raised eyebrow—at most, you'll be amazed by what these folks did and who they really were.

Now, let me introduce you to Weldon Kees.

Weldon Kees was a poet in the fifties alongside the finger-snapping, beret-wearing Beatniks, but this guy was his own Midwestern man. And he wasn't just a poet, but a painter, filmmaker, and experimental photographer.

I'll be up front about Kees: there's every chance he set out from Nebraska, parked his car near the Golden Gate Bridge on July 18, 1955, and smiled as he intentionally sank to the bottom of the bay. He probably felt a wider spectrum of feelings than the rest of us—like those folks who can see an extra shade of yellow. He was living at the height of the Beat Generation, guys like Kerouac setting the world on fire, and Kees wasn't really that sort of jazz-influenced, wild-eyed hipster with a boatload of bennies pumping through his veins. He wasn't a buttoned-down dude, but he may have felt like a poet without a posse, so to speak. It's conceivable that Kees bid this cruel world farewell and leaped into the abyss.

Still: an acquaintance swore up and down she saw him hanging out with a hot blonde around the Big Easy in '62. A fellow writer recounted tossing back tequilas with Kees in Mexico years after the poet disappeared. Over time, the legend sprouted from a seed to a beanstalk—Weldon Kees was alive and living like Elvis in East Hullabaloo.

I made that up, I don't think there is an East Hullabaloo.

Even if Kees jumped off that bridge to a watery grave, he was unintentionally brilliant in the run up to his vanishing.

First, there's the part we have no control over: this guy was handsome, artistically gifted, and charismatic. It's no wonder his disappearance might stir up romantic imaginations, but whatever window these imaginations had into his life was substantially tinted.

Kees told one friend he might just start fresh south of the border. That was a cinch back in the day; the border-crossing procedure was a friendly nod and raise of your Schlitz as you rumbled into Juarez. Kees could've easily learned a little Español and made his way without much start-up capital.

On the other hand, he hinted he was fine with ending it all, too. He may or may not fit the bill of a guy who sought a new life free of all the bullshit Eisenhower's America was throwing into the fan. Either way, Kees achieved mythical status prior to departure.

You'd think such a missing presence would send droves of cops, fans, and ex-girlfriends on his trail. Calling back to those opaque windows, Weldon Kees threw some shade into the sitch. In his apartment they found his cat (very much alive), a pair of red socks (in the sink of all places), but no wallet, watch, or bank account passbook. Damned if his sleeping bag wasn't missing, too.

However, he had a sizable stack of 1955-ish greenbacks in the bank that he never touched again.

While Weldon left us all floundering and flummoxed, he left an important lesson for you free-spirited, pre-disappeared: leave 'em guessing themselves into a tizzy over what the hell happened to you.

Leave socks in the sink, dishes in the closet! It's all about the art of misdirection, Ricky Jay. Make sure they're always looking in the wrong place. Take all your camping equipment, build a site in your local park, then drive away. What matters is that no one figures you out.

Now let's skip back to a post-World War II mystery: a dude with a dancer's build and poison within. A poster boy for identity eradication: the Somerton Man.

A snazzily dressed, well-built, nice-looking guy lay on the beach, his head propped against the seawall as if he was merely taking a snooze under the Australian summer sun in December of 1948. Except the guy was a goner. And no one knew who the hell he was even nearly seventy years later. This man did a bang-up job of leaving his proverbial footprints close enough to the tide that they were washed clean away.

CASE IN POINT

Herein lies the tale of the Tamam Shud Case—aka the Somerton Man.

Okay, so the guy may have been a spy. That doesn't invalidate his story here, no way—because the truth is, *compañero*, we are moving into territory where spies are the men and women who led the way.

The Somerton Man was in his forties and no stranger to the gym. His fashionable getup contained nothing to give the perplexed Aussie cops any idea as to who he was. Just his essentials: gum, cigarettes, and an American-made comb.

Big whoop at first peek, right? Keep those eyeballs sharp and excited; I'm not done with this guy.

Our unidentified friend is hauled from the beach to the coroner and it's discovered he was at the pinnacle of health. At the time, science available in the land of the koala, the kangaroo, and the really big knife couldn't determine the exact kind of poison, but the coroner uttered something of a puzzled, "sure looks like poison to me, mate."

Attempts to track the guy's fingerprints flopped (and for you spring chickens reading this, DNA wasn't a thing back then), but police eventually managed to match him up with a locker at a train station in Adelaide. In the locker, they found a suitcase full of clothes and an odd set of tools that the investigators linked to merchant marine use. So maybe he was a handyman sailing under the Jolly Roger, a pirate who'd made a few enemies before winding up Down Under?

Our buddy Somerton Man had torn the tags from nearly everything, but those eagle-eyed officers managed to find the name "T. Keane" scribbled in a couple of places. To further twist the pickle, it became obvious after deeper digging that this guy wasn't the Keane in question. Dead ends are all anyone ever got with Somerton Man.

What about that weird phrase, "Tamam shud?" Sewn into the lining of one of his pants pockets, police found a sheet of paper inscribed with the words "Tamam shud." The phrase means "completed" or "finished" and comes from a book of ancient Persian poems, *The Rubáiyát of Omar Khayyám*. And if you're not yet hooked by the mystery of this lone dude's name, the enigma continues.

People love an unsolved story, especially one with a creepy code attached. Hence the Zodiac Killer's inclusion on the *Billboard* Top 100 of favorite serial killer mysteries. While Zodiac's code was cracked, Somerton Man left one that has yet to be deciphered. That phrase "Tamam Shud" wasn't just a reference to a book, it was torn from the pages of a specific copy. Investigators found that copy, and written into the inside cover was a string of capital letters that look like nonsense. There are theories galore, but in the end, no one really knows.

Perhaps the Somerton Man was a displaced spy or had been one in the past. Sounds like something someone of that type might be motivated to do, right? Completely clean up the record and leave only a fine-looking corpse? Lesson here is: make sure your mystery eclipses your identity.

On the sentimental side, he might've been an average military guy who came to Adelaide for an old love and ended up rejected by her—some deep cut from all the sad fallout of World War II. Whoever this guy was, the way he obscured his trail to that beach was ingenious. He performed a total erasure by leaving unanswerable questions in his wake.

As you factor him into our conversation, remember this: neither Somerton Man nor Weldon Kees had to contend with the World Wide Web. They were escaping from a *way* less connected life than the one we're in now. Sure, there were ways to track people, but back then you didn't even have to be a particularly clever liar to evade anyone who might be hunting you; it was usually as simple as a few carefully placed, simple lies and a dose of solitude. You're going to have to escape from the Usain Bolt–equivalent of a black widow, while these guys were battling a garden spider with the Web-equivalent of erectile dysfunction.

We're stuck with a universe of connected databases and metadata and algorithms and other sophisticated cyber-jargon. Let's give a respectful nod to the ghosts of Mr. Kees and Mr. Somerton Man and admit that if either man's story occurred today, we'd probably end up with more answers to our questions. There would be traces on social media, little snippets of info in online profiles. Even photographs forgotten on a Myspace account might be enough for a clever researcher to put two and two together and find a real name.

So let's move on up to a much more recent case, a guy who's still alive and kicking. A man whom friends called Clark and figured for a rich New England weirdo. His buried story, though, was a lot more fun, until it took a turn.

Clark Rockefeller, Who Was Not a Rockefeller

The completely banana-pants story of Clark Rockefeller is a lesson for anyone who has ever dreamed of simply becoming a new person in a new place. And Clarkasaurus Rex, who is the modern king of this thing we're talking about, did it in style.

Unfortunately, Clark Rockefeller's story is not the hero's journey I'd like it to be. Clark had a real gift for not only getting off the grid, but for ensuring the grid forgot him completely—and living a seemingly normal life the entire time. That part is pivotal to our purposes here.

Admittedly, in the end, he wasn't exactly a "good guy." You're about to hear a combination case study of a nearly perfect disappearance and a sinister cautionary tale.

Clark's name first hit the news as a suspect in a kidnapping case. Even then, he was the sort of accused gent I might have readily defended during my time at the bar. Poor guy only got supervised visitation with his young daughter a few times a year—a daughter who otherwise lived overseas. Clark loved that kid, and while on one of those visits, he grabbed his daughter and fled in a waiting SUV. Dad of the Year, right? The love of a parent knows no bounds!

At first, Clark's was a typical story of a parent who had grown desperate and snapped under the pressures of a post-divorce life. Then—insert the sound of a record scratch here—things got weird.

As the cops started looking for our buddy Clark, they quickly learned that he was not a rogue product of *that* Rockefeller family. Clark wasn't some outlier from old money, the kind of rich guy who shakes diamonds like salt crystals onto his Salade Niçoise, well-versed enough to chat about the conditions of the surf off the Cape. No, this guy was . . . well, he was someone else entirely.

When he was arrested, he was nondescript Chip Smith, living in an apartment he'd purchased in Baltimore. Chip Smith would be the end of the line for this guy, who had been wearing a slew of different identities since the late 1970s.

Before he was Clark Rockefeller, he was Christopher Chichester. If you've ever seen *Gilligan's Island*, you might remember the rich old guy who lived in the third bamboo hut on the left on that show: Thurston Howell III. If you spoke to him on the phone, you'd suspect Christopher Chichester was a dead-ringer for Thurston Howell.

He rented a guesthouse from the elderly Didi Sohus in San Marino, California. Didi had a son named Jon and a daughter-in-law named Linda. Chichester, Jon, and Linda all disappeared in 1985. Chichester bobbed back up on the grid a few years later in New England, trying to sell a truck registered to Jon Sohus. The buyer smelled something fishy (and it wasn't just the prevailing scent of clam chowder hanging in the Northeastern air), so the transaction didn't go down. Chichester vanished, and our buddy Clark was born.

If you're already impressed with the guy—let's start by looking at what he did right.

On the surface: no matter his current identity, he always committed to his shtick du jour. As Chichester, he presented himself as an old-money aristocrat, allegedly hinting at ties to English royalty for good measure. He purportedly worked in the television industry, and even had his own community cable access show. A regular silk-stocking man about town.

In another way, he kept his life very low key. Rented from a private citizen, likely got by on charm and didn't even have to sign a lease, I'd bet.

But it all fell apart in Connecticut, the moment he realized he might have made a misstep trying to sell the truck of a missing man. He dropped out of sight and remodeled himself into Clark Rockefeller.

But we aren't really digging into the creepy miracles and mysteries of the Clark Rockefeller saga unless we get back to his true origin story. He wasn't even an American.

When he first arrived in the land of Stars and Stripes in 1979, the Clarkster's name was Christian Gerhartsreiter. Of the Bavarian Gerhartsreiters, in Germany. He was an exchange student in high school, and our Mozart of misdirection seems to have begun concocting a plan even then. He studied American culture. He was a big fan of *Gilligan's Island,* and studied Thurston Howell III's uppercrust accent, not realizing it was a parody.

The man who would become Clark started enacting his plan in 1981 with a green card marriage. Then, he simply Anglicized his birth name to Chris Gerhart. But something was still amiss, so he evolved from caterpillar into Chichester.

To bottom-line this thing: even in a steadily connecting modern world, the man managed to evade any detection for thirty years.

If he hadn't finally found a heart where his kid was concerned, he might still be tooling around New England today as that blue-blooded Rockefeller cousin.

This guy had a scheme ready at every turn. Rockefeller married the mother of his child in a ceremony that was legally meaningless. There wasn't an actual marriage license filed in the county where it occurred (but I'm sure the reception was very nice). Once he was in the marriage, he convinced his wife to file taxes as a single woman, and he told her accountant that he was her brother. This man instinctively knew how to evade detection.

The kicker is: after 1985, he had a lot more motivation to be very good at making sure he was never brushed by the long arm of the law.

Remember how that couple, Jon and Linda Sohus, disappeared around the same time Christopher Chichester lit out from San Marino? Never to be heard from again until Chichester tried to sell Jon's truck in Connecticut?

The authorities found Jon Sohus's bones and a whole lot of other evidence Rockefeller didn't realize he'd scattered around. In 2009, a jury found Clark guilty of Sohus's murder. He won't be out of jail till he's a very old man.

Let's have a refreshing glass of cucumber water and review: if there's one thing linking all these disappearances so far, it's confusion. These gentlemen all gave anyone chasing them a giant tossed salad of conflicting information. One guy, maybe he committed suicide. Maybe he went off to Mexico. The other guy just removed evidence of who he might have been (not to mention: he added a creepy code to the mix, and who doesn't love that). And the third guy—his fatal flaw was loving his kid too much. And murder. That didn't help, either.

Then there's Joe, the guy who got it right. As we sit

here right now, in our undisclosed locations, nobody really knows who the hell Joe was. Old Joe did everything his way, including shuffling off this mortal coil. On one hand his story is kind of sad. On the other, he might be the best example of a guy who did exactly what we're talking about and made it work like a damned charm.

Joseph Newton Chandler III

This guy. Up front, here's why I thought he was a great case study for any seeker looking for the golden key out of their crappy life: he managed to survive, thrive, and then when it looked as though he might be in a situation in which he was compromised, Joey Newts fled and didn't even leave a proper fingerprint behind.

His name wasn't Joseph Newton Chandler III, obviously. No, the owner of that moniker was taking a dirt nap some thirty-three years when our man applied for a social security card in his name in 1978. Our hero likely roamed cemeteries or maybe even knew the original Joe Chandler (who died when he was only a kid). At the time the real Joe passed, social security wasn't fully in effect and no number had ever been attached to the name. So new Joe really didn't have to work too hard in the late

'70s to pick up a deceased kid's birth certificate and tack a social onto the package.

What's awesome about the new Joe Chandler? The guy was really, really boring.

Think about it: he acquired the basic papers he needed to rent an apartment or get a job in 1978 and then—zip. Never heard from until he died, a suicide in a Cleveland apartment in 2003.

His switcheroo from whomever he'd been to Joe wasn't discovered until after he was dead. He'd been diagnosed with a dire form of cancer and decided to handle things his own way. He left behind over $80,000 in the bank, and the usual legal aftermath of death took its course. Investigators started looking for his heirs. But he had no heirs. And then—they discovered he wasn't Joe, after all.

The mystery grew greater because he'd left specific instructions to cremate his remains. His remains naturally included his fingers. Which held his fingerprints. And before you say "You don't need fingers to find fingerprints,"—puzzled investigators couldn't find any prints to dust in his apartment, because it appeared he'd wiped it all down.

I'd like to take a little moment of silence to marvel at that. The guy had lived in his apartment for years, but no one could find a single usable print. And at the time he died, the cremation also made sure no one was getting the guy's DNA, either. Case closed. Well, sort of.

A U.S. Marshal who investigated our guy told a reporter about eleven years after Joe offed himself that the fake Mr. Chandler had "lived the perfect life of someone on the run."

He wasn't wrong.

Joey Newts had no close friends. He let a few coworkers in just enough for them to learn some of his quirks—one guy told of Joe driving from Cleveland to Maine to shop, only to turn around and go home when he couldn't find a parking space—but Joe had no bosom buddies. No true companions.

Joey Newts made no waves. Even though cops trying to figure out who the guy was have expressed suspicions he was a fugitive, Joey Newts didn't commit any crimes that anyone knew of between 1978 and 2003. Clean as a whistle. He might have had a girlfriend or two over the years, sure, but he generally kept his head down and his feet shuffling along. He ended up being remembered as a slightly weird but low-key dude.

Joey Newts was just about the perfect case of how to change your identity and get away with it.

I'm not letting you in on all the fun if I don't touch on the nature of the legend that grew up around old Joe after his long con became national news.

One theory about Joseph Newton Chandler III: he was the Zodiac Killer. There's a good reason. In the few photos available of the guy (another good point to remember: be camera-shy), particularly anything made for an ID, it's pretty easy to match his face up with some famous old suspect sketches of the code-writing maniac.

There were a lot of theories about Zodiac, and one was that he had engineering knowledge and, of course, that he was living in California. Joey Newts apparently lived in the Golden State at some point, and he had engineering skill. On top of all that, who but a wanted serial killer would have reason to not just disappear, but completely erase any trace of who he had been before?

Some also thought he could be D. B. Cooper. Cooper was a similarly built guy—thin, average height—who jumped out of a plane with $200,000 in ransom money in 1971 and was never heard from again. Straight up vanished into the great northwest. Cooper had the means and the reason to get the hell out of whatever he was up to before he took his wild ride, and who's to say he didn't lay low, trying on a few new names and lives before settling down as Joe?

I don't really buy it. A thrill killer and a skyjacker? Those are a couple of guys who love to live on the edge. They probably need that adrenaline jolt to keep their tickers ticking. Joe got his new name in 1978 and then played it cool for a very long time. This guy wasn't looking for fun: he was looking to be forgotten.

The ladies have been left out in my little recitation of theses known unknowns. See, I saved Lori Ruff for last intentionally. We'll get into more details about detaching from your old grid and what that really means for you in a few, but I had to bring up Lori first because the late Ms. Ruff may have accidentally been one of the best of this little murderer's row of Does. Accidentally, because she wasn't the most mentally sound of the bunch. Normally, I'd insist that this requires a pretty cool, clear head. Lori had some issues and wasn't very organized, but she's the most recent case study I know about in which someone slipped off the grid and managed to stay off, even after she was dead and fingerprints and DNA were easily available.

Lori Erica Ruff

Not to speak ill of the dead, but Texan Lori Ruff was pretty obviously a woman splintering into a million little pieces when she died by her own hand in 2010. She may have seemed like someone who had it all, at one point.

A tall woman, very intelligent. But by the time she killed herself, her marriage had completely shattered, and her soon-to-be-former in-laws were seriously considering taking out a restraining order against her. She was incredibly secretive about herself, but obsessed with her husband's genealogy. She was also hyperprotective of her child, and refused to let others hold the baby at all.

Lori was strange, but no one knew just how strange until she died and they started poking around, trying to figure out exactly who she was.

Before she was Lori Ruff, she was Lori Kennedy.

Before she was Lori Kennedy, she was Becky Sue Turner. And here's where we learn she was kind of a soul mate to old Joey Newts: the real Becky Sue Turner had been dead since 1971. At some point seventeen years after little Becky Sue said the long good-night, a woman acquired her birth certificate and took it to Idaho, where she snagged a state ID.

That was Lori's first stepping stone. She now had a plausible birth record and a legit state identification. She took these promising nuggets to the great state of Texas and pulled another awesome camouflaging move: she changed her name again. She became Lori Kennedy via a legal name change.

Honestly, this was a boss move on many levels. Lori

had quickly put two full layers between her current identity and whatever name her biological parents had bestowed upon her.

After that, she blitzed through a GED and went to college, firmly establishing an impressive new life for herself.

There's no need to get into the tall grass about why this mystery woman broke down and took her own life. What's interesting from my perspective—and yours, too, I'd guess, given this talk we're having—is how after Lori was gone, very little about what she left behind gave any clue as to who she might have been. She left behind mysterious scribblings: an attorney's name (he said he never knew her), the words "North Hollywood," and some info that seemed to hint at legal trouble. Someone also uncovered an example of just how carefully Lori had concealed herself: she'd set up a mail-forwarding service in Nevada that kicked correspondences to her actual address in Texas.

I couldn't find any evidence anyone ever knew who Lori really was. Considering she was alive and kicking well after the Internet began making it seem impossible to hide from anyone, that's a hell of an accomplishment. The sad thing about Lori's story is while we could easily suspect all these guys of being on the run from their own nefarious past, there's something to be said about running from the demons inside you. Lori may have escaped from any prior crimes or abusers, but it seems as though she was never quite able to find peace within herself.

Always at Orange

If my goal is to get your mojo working toward a new life, I'm not doing my due diligence unless I note that the stories I just told you have several common elements and one of them is death. Specifically: suicide comes up a lot.

So let's be real. Red meat, bitter coffee time: this shit is tough to do. I'm getting this out there right now because we've got more of the fun and fascinating world of getting the hell out of Dodge to explore. Keeping your head down, not popping up like a prairie dog to sniff the air and get the attention of The Man: it's a full-time job.

So, think back on your police training (if not yours, then someone else's) and keep track of your alertness level using Cooper's Colors: white, yellow, orange, red.

Former Marine Jeff Cooper broke down combat

mind-set into four states: "white" (relaxed and oblivious) to "red" (hyperaware and focused on a target). The in-between levels are "yellow," which is the average person's state of mind when driving, let's say. Relaxed enough, but alert and aware. Up from that is "orange."

Condition orange is a state of readiness. You're pretty sure something's coming, and you have an exit route and a go-bag you can grab the moment you are certain you have to skedaddle.

Everyday humans who haven't left another life behind exist pretty much day to day in white to yellow zones. In an unwelcome environment, they're at orange. If they get mugged, it goes up to red.

Here's the thing about performing your one-night-only vanishing act: you're always going to be at orange from here on out.

When I sleep I guess I must dial my awareness down to the white condition. No choice there. Maybe yellow, if every bump in the night snaps me awake in a drenching sweat. But from the time I wake—and this has to be true for everyone in this boat, even if they're under witness protection or something official like that—it's orange all the time, until I lose consciousness again.

Simply put: jumping off the grid and becoming another person on paper, in a new place, with a new career, you name it—well it involves a constant level of pucker factor.

Fiction for Popular Consumption

It has occurred to me that a number of people interested in this pathway into a new life might be well-served if they figure out a plausible cover story to aid in leaving behind some kind of smoke screen.

Think about the alternative. One of the quickest ways to get some very unwanted attention after you exit stage left might be leaving behind a juicy mystery. That's all well and good once you've kicked the bucket and joined Joey Newts in John Doe Purgatory to eat cobbler and laugh at the named world—but my friend, it's contrary to your purposes if what you want is another few decades kicking around this terra firma under a different identity.

Lie Like a Rug

To put a razor-sharp point on the proceedings: one of your biggest projects is to lie. Lie often and well. It's vital to do so as you're ramping up to leave, because you need to create a distinct pattern of deception. Part of getting away as scot-free as possible is creating an effective disinformation campaign.

Hey, with casual friends and acquaintances—coworkers, people at church, the cute chick you always wave to at the supermarket—that's not so hard. It gets stickier when we talk about close friends and, most of all, family.

It's not as simple as setting up an automated e-mail responder that tells folks you're going on a Caribbean Cruise for the next two weeks. You need something longer term than that.

The following hints and suggestions won't be of much use to you lucky singletons and others who have no close family to answer to. If you're married or partnered up in any fashion, the following is a bit more in your ballpark. Remember that these are just the themes you need to improvise on. I can only lay down the tracks, it's up to you to riff.

World Travels. This one is tried-and-true for folks with fewer connections, and I can guarantee it has been used by some to give themselves a cushion of time between disappearance and investigation. The solid tip for any family man or woman who wants to try this cover on for size is: don't make your fictional gallivanting to points unknown appealing to your partner.

Let's say Jeff from Oregon is setting up a changeover to becoming Dave from Kentucky. Sadly, he's got to leave his partner Dana behind, since having more than one person on the run from a past life is pretty much a guarantee it won't work. Now, let's say our pal Jeff knows Dana absolutely hates cold weather. Snow falls, Dana locks the doors. If I were Jeff in this scenario, I might dream up plans to embark on one of those chilly jaunts to Antarctica. Depending on his skill set, he could even fake a job opportunity. Someone who really loathes the cold is likely to pass on that adventure, and not think twice about lack of correspondence until a fake notice comes from the snowy wastes in the form of an official message indicating poor Jeff died in some horrible ice-floe surfing incident. I'm spitballing, of course.

The weakness of the vacation cover is always going to be how appealing it sounds to any loved ones who might normally expect to go along for the ride. So unless you engineer the deception appropriately and make it sound miserable, this isn't the option to use.

Language Immersion. I'm pretty fond of this one. It's simple: pick a language—like French, Russian, Mandarin, or Spanish—and make every effort to set up a plausible scenario that has you jetting off to whatever exotic locale is appropriate.

Maybe it's a Cold War childhood talking, but the idea of saying I'm heading to Moscow for four weeks of deep immersion in Russian sounds pretty cool. Plus, you get to seem real scholarly; people will be impressed. Might even get you laid a few times before you go. The kicker with this is: you may need to be kind of brainy in the first place. If people don't think of you as a lifelong academic, someone with an interest arguing with Ivan and Mischa over bites of pickles and herring, the foreign language gambit will only raise suspicion. Still, it's a slightly more solid option for some than a mysterious cruise to a far-off land. As with so many recommendations, use with care and caution.

A Romantic Gambit. If you're single, this one is almost perfect. I call it "The Canadian Girlfriend Maneuver," and it's not just for those unfortunate young men who feel a pressure to stay in the closet. It's as simple as saying you've fallen in love with someone in another nation and your heart can't take another moment living long distance. You may need to set up a pretty complex charade. Make it look as if you're working on a passport, residency visa, the works. You could even invent evidence of the relationship (fake online profiles, maybe pay a model to pose with you in photos). Once that's all established: hit the road with the blessing of all around you, because who wants to get in the way of true love?

Contingency Plans

In all the cases we've looked at, we were examining scenarios that require time and careful planning. The problem with needing to ditch your old life and identity for a new one is this: sometimes troubles aren't slowly seeping floods, they're by-God tsunamis threatening to swallow you up mere moments after the precipitating earthquake. If you're a federal witness and you've decided to drop a dime on some major kingpin, for example, the nice boys at the DEA or FBI or wherever could squirrel you right off the grid in the space of a few hours, leaving your house like the creepily deserted *Mary Celeste* plopped in the middle of the suburbs, with nearly fresh food still on the dinner table.

That probably won't be you. But what if you discover the need to leave is immediate and pressing? And what if you don't have a lot of time to plan?

There are, I have to admit, a good number of ways to skin this cat. For the casual reader who currently has no plans to leave the grid at all but maybe, just maybe, has the niggling feeling they should be prepared for any possibility, I'll list some smart skills to acquire and a couple of contingency supplies.

Supplies

Survivalists get a bad rap from the unprepared world. They're portrayed as unhinged and paranoid, certain that doom is just around the corner. When you see survival-obsessed characters in a movie, they're usually presented like lunatic rednecks interested in wearing your skin for warmth through the long nuclear winter that they'll be waiting out in their creepy bomb shelters.

There is probably a percentage of survivalists who fit that bill, just as there is likely a small percentage of attorneys who also moonlight as male strippers nicknamed Kevin Cosplay. But a ton of these folks are everyday people who just want to face calamity in a realistic way. They're the well-prepared students of life, realists who understand that when times get tough, people can get desperate and dangerous. There's nothing wrong with keeping an earthquake kit in your house and a hatchet in your car—as long as you don't plan to use the latter when gridlocked traffic starts stirring up the road rage within you.

Anyone who is looking to exit their identity can learn a little something from the world of the well-prepared, especially if you're that unfortunate civilian facing some kind of sudden-onset personal disaster.

Kitty. Not a cat, though they're perfectly nice little balls of fur and fangs. Something we already talked about—money, honey. There's a consistent theme for you: save the hell up. See if you can set aside a ten-spot a day for the next two months, and boom, you've got $600 you can grab in an emergency.

Bug-out Bag. If you're going to buy just one thing, buy this—or put one together on your own. Select a big box store and go to the department where they sell the fun stuff like desert camo underwear, for folks who like to run around in the desert . . . in their underwear, I guess. Many sell a go-bag. It's a backpack or duffel, and it comes prefilled with an awesome assortment of crap sure to appeal to your inner Boy or Girl Scout. Stuff like a battery- and solar-operated flashlight, waterproof matches, a hand-crank radio, a knife, duct tape, first aid kit, and some dry food designed to be edible even after a nuclear blast.

A premade go-bag might cost up to $500 depending on where you get it and how extensive it is. If you want to assemble your own, analyze what comes in the pre-packaged go-bags and see what's missing. Maybe you'll want to make sure you've packed your own camouflage-colored underwear.

Dirt-Simple Disguise. Barring some really hard-to-hide feature like a vestigial twin, I'm pretty sure most people don't realize just how quickly and easily they can disguise themselves well enough to evade surveillance.

Your gender doesn't matter: nothing like putting on a simple ball cap and a pair of shades to suddenly and simply obscure your identity. Keep those on hand; they make light, collapsible ball caps now that fit easily in a jacket pocket. Or, just wear a hoodie with the hood pulled up, if the weather is right. Another tip I've read about is reversible clothing. There's a limit to how much of that you can find, and you might consider learning some tailoring skills to make your own, but it could be incredibly useful to double your wardrobe.

If you're in the unfortunate position of having to rough it because your need to drop off the grid was too immediate to lay down the groundwork for a new identity, you are probably going to need some of the following skills, which are sometimes called Urban Survival Skills.

Dumpster Diving. Yeah, I've already touched on this. No, I'm not fond of it at all, but let's face it—people throw out a lot of stuff, and some of it is actually useful. More than that, just as I mentioned early on, there is information in that there garbage. Let's say you've had to make your emergency bug-out and fled your abode, and for some reason it only then occurs to you that you might need a temporary new identity. Probably gonna find all you need right there in your new best friend's trash. Maybe double-stock that bug-out backpack with as much long-lasting food as you can, so you won't be forced to snack like a well-dressed raccoon.

Straight-up Burglary. I'm not advocating stealing for the sake of stealing. But let's face it, there are specific situations where it may even be judicious to briefly bust in and make yourself at home in a residence that is not your own. Rather than instruct you in the actual art of burglary—which is very straightforward unless you want to get sophisticated and learn lock picking, etc.— I'll just note for the record that there have been a few folks who have made an art of this and lived off the grid for years doing it.

Caveat: these folks had to confine themselves to living in the woods, so maybe only consider this if you are comfortable with the fresh air, the forest, and the bears.

First there was the North Pond Hermit, also known as "Chris." He managed to live for three decades off the grid in the woods of Central Maine, an area that is all green, glorious, moose dropping-filled woods. But Chris managed, even in Maine's nasty winters, by being a perfectly practical burglar. He never even built a campfire. About forty times a year, give or take, from 1986 to 2013, Chris would burglarize residences—mostly vacation cabins—for supplies. He was no master criminal. He took food, the necessary kitchen implements needed to prepare it, and fuel in the form of propane. He might also grab a book or two just because you can only commune with the ghosts of the New England timberland for so long before they have to return to their home inside Stephen King's head. He took clothes, too—but just what he needed. Chris was so deft about all this that some people didn't even realize he'd burgled them at all.

Second guy who managed to make it off the grid and stay wasn't quite as benign as gentle Chris. Troy—again, first name only—survived a solid decade well out of society's hair in the Utah mountains. Again, a seriously forbidding environment, if you're looking for a pattern to these semi-successful stories of staying out of sight. Go somewhere nobody wants to look for you.

Troy said "see ya" to society some time in 2004. He was on parole at the time. From that moment until his capture in 2014, Troy remained coy with the rest of humanity, stating that it wasn't that he didn't like people, he just didn't want to be near them. Troy managed by kind of colonizing remote vacation cabins. He'd live in them. Sometimes he did just like Chris and took only what he needed to survive. You know, essentials like whiskey. Other times, Troy shot up the residences and left vaguely threatening notes. Rangers and cops finally tracked him down, then snuck up on him quietly, clad in snow shoes.

Once again, don't try this at home. More specifically, at other peoples' homes. It's illegal, and sadly there's one fewer great lawyer out there these days to represent you if you get caught.

Hacking for Fun and Profit. No, you are not going to learn the inner secrets of hacking from the former Saul Goodman. Just as I didn't hip you to the how-tos of burglary, I sure can't tell you how to steal passwords by casually browsing books at a library while eyeballing someone using a computer at a desk nearby, or that there is easily available software right there on the Internet that will grab all the keystrokes off a public computer, including any number of passwords and bank accounts. I will say that lessons for absolute beginners in the basics of unauthorized computer use are all over the place, including the World Wide Web. So a smidge of knowledge about computer-based chicanery could be a useful tool to have in your kit.

At bare minimum, you could use the password-eyeballing trick to do what's otherwise a real no-no when you're on the run, and get on the Internet to figure out what's up in your old life. If the cops are hitting up your friends on social media with questions, distributing photos of your face, that kind of thing.

By the way, since we all have handheld supercomputers in our pockets these days, it's worth pointing out that they're totally hackable, too.

A phone like that is a double-edged sword. For the grid-skipper fleeing troubles aplenty, a tutorial on how to get into a "borrowed" smart phone is pure gold. However, owning a phone like that can be a lot of trouble, too. In a little bit we'll get into the phone issue in more depth, because these fine little companions we keep in our pockets to see weather conditions and pornography on tiny screens could end up hanging the desperate traveler out to dry.

We've traveled down the muddy, rutted road of the rapid bug-out as much as we have time for right now. What it comes down to is planning. Even if everything I'm putting down is for entertainment purposes only, don't take it for granted that one day you may need some of this advice.

The bug-out bag, for example: what harm is it to order one today then pop it under the bed, or in the back of the closet? Sure, you might be in the middle of a move years from now, find it, and laugh at your paranoia, but an asteroid might drop on the closest major city tomorrow. If that happens, everyone squiring shih tzus and toddlers through the suburbs in their compact SUVs will be screwed, but you'll be the smart one with a few days' supply of food, water purifying tablets, and a cozy mylar blanket tucked into a pack on your back.

Most folks aren't worried about an actual dinosaur destroyer of an asteroid, though—they're worried about whatever figurative asteroid of trouble might be shooting their way. Whatever sinks your boat, I hope you're ready with a life vest and some dried apricots.

Travel Advisories

There's always a roadblock somewhere. Let's say you've done just about everything right, so far. You carefully picked out a dead guy or gal and copped their birth certificate. You quietly acquired a state-issued identification card. Then let's say you locked down lodging—perhaps a weekly hotel to start, paid for in cash or with a pre-paid debit card. You are on your way. Maybe you're at a point where you're focused on laying down a firmer foundation in your new home. The kind of thing that takes a little time and attention.

Here's where I hit you with a little bit of cold water:

Roadblocks. Actual real ones and a few mental speed bumps as well.

Here's a scenario, a very simple one. Say you've settled into innocuous, out-of-the-way neighborhood X on the outskirts of middle-of-nowhere town B. Very good place to disappear. Maybe you've been living under your new name for several months and have grown . . . comfortable. Anyone would. No, you're not letting your guard down. Digitally, you've completely left your old online persona behind. You have a landline phone under your new name and you've made sure that number's unlisted. If you were an author, you'd fall somewhere between "Salinger" and "Pynchon" on the publicity scale.

One morning, you wake up feeling pretty good and want to celebrate with a half-dozen donuts. Just because you've taken on a new name and identity doesn't mean you have to lay low and hide in your darkened split-level ranch all the time, right?

You head into town to get your Homer Simpson on—and when you come back, you're met by a blockade at the only road leading into your neighborhood. There you are, carrying a driver's license that the first friendly officer who stops your ride might examine carefully for signs of fraudulence.

If the roadblock is for a certain criminal element known to reside near you (drug dealer, wanted felon who happened to live one street over, etc.) it may be no big deal! Quick glance, the appropriate hologram burned into the ID's plastic coating, and you're good to go. You're not what's on the menu today.

But then again, what if you're not waved right along? No matter what you've heard about duty-sworn officers of the law, most of them are not easily nor readily swayed by a half-dozen donuts. Hell, not even a full dozen. You may well be boned after you've only just begun, my friend. The most innocuous irritation—a routine checkpoint meant to roust one lone weed dealer—can potentially trip you up.

And here we come to that cold, hard catch-22 about life off the grid: just because you're paranoid doesn't mean they're not out to get you.

So: the house you found to rent from a landlord who didn't care about background-checking you because you had the cash to offer up front? The one in a neighborhood with a one-road entrance? *Who the hell normally plans around that kind of thing?* No one but criminals and volcanologists. Folks with all their proper papers have no need to worry about how many roads lead away from their pleasantly beige home base at the end of a cul-de-sac. But you? You have to brace yourself for the unexpected catastrophic eruption.

The closed-lipped suburbs where no one expects a

lone wolf to attend the bi-monthly HOA meetings seem like a great place to hide out, but it might be more wise to invest in the anonymous week-by-week extended-stay motels that sit right off a major interstate and usually offer a free continental breakfast between six and nine AM. If that's too much excitement for you (and you can't convince yourself that the highway sounds like a sooth-ing river lulling you to sleep every night), at least make it a habit to study the maps of whichever neighbor-bland 'hood you've decided to retire to. A few different routes in and out, only the most tasteful graffiti—why plop down in a heavily monitored neighborhood if the main thing you're trying to do is avoid attention? Keep in mind that cops will run background checks on witnesses to crimes, too.

I'm being discouraging, I know. But—and this is a big old but—it doesn't have to be this way. Just make sure to align yourself with the philosophical styling of "K.I.S.S."

We all want to rock and roll all night and party every day, but I'm not referring to the pyrotechnic-loving, blood-spitting brothers Paul, Gene, Peter, and Ace. I'm talking about that old military tenet of "Keep it simple, stupid." It's always a good idea to examine your options and take the cleanest, most simple one. When launch-ing a second life under a new name, you need to take

Occam's razor and whittle everything down to the basics.

We're talking money, shelter, sustenance. Go someplace out of the way, distant, unsung—but unlike the cabin-plundering hermits I told you about, don't drill that down to a permanent tent in the woods. Most people can't handle that life.

Gather All the Intelligence About You. Spy stuff again. The moment you lock in on a new destination to reboot your existence, the first thing you should do is doctorate-level research on that locale. If you've never been the best student, fix that! And here's the great thing: the Internet is a huge help in such an endeavor. Become a historian, cartographer, and an avid fan of the soap opera starring your new neighbors. Fact is, pretty much anyone can utilize a search engine and gather enough data about even the smallest town to fill an entire home library.

Unless you take the very chancy chance of hiring someone to map out the whole deal in advance, then you will have to be the hunter-gatherer of your own intelligence. Put together aerial views, stats about demographics, income, and crime. Read letters to the editor in the local paper. Target the part of town where you want to live. Remember: you don't want flashy; you want bland. Avoid mansions; avoid broken windows.

Don't take it personally—this choice won't make you bland at all! Doing the whole "new identity" thing automatically puts you in the category of "Very Interesting Person" for life. Which brings me to my next point . . .

Don't Be So Damn Interesting. Whoops, sorry. Are you a charismatic character? The kind of gal or guy who warms up the room the moment you arrive at the party? Take it from Saul, friend: put that light under a bushel, ASAP. Don't be colorful. Look back on the folks I've already told you about who remain total mysteries to this very day—what ties them together? I'll tell you: they were boring as hell. Remember Joey Newts? From 1978 till 2003, he could have won his workplace's award for Most Vanilla Employee. Dial down that inner party monster, and channel your inner introvert.

On one level this seems easy: just don't talk to people. Restrict daily communication to the necessities related to whatever practical business you're up to, and only that. Say you grab a job as the lowly attendant at the morgue, one of those guys who helps haul the dead bodies around. Whatever you do, don't start making observations about the transitory nature of existence. Avoid deep thoughts. Embrace the shallow. If someone says the local single-A baseball team is interesting, do not debate this. Try not to have polarizing opinions about things. This is not the time to reach deep into the recesses of your mathematics degree and go all *Money-ball* on your coworkers. Your only reply should be, "Yeah, baseball's cool, man." Your safety and anonymity is at stake. It's shocking how easily that can turn on its head when you become a person of interest to the interested persons around you.

The Three *R*'s—Routine, Routine, Routine. The moment you've settled anywhere for any length of time and mapped out your typical day, just stick with it. Aspire to be like Mr. Rogers, who came home at the same time every day, swapped his jacket for a sweater, and slid on his comfortable tennis shoes. And you know what? Every day was a beautiful day in his neighborhood.

This can be a little confusing if you've been under surveillance in the past, I know—because a great tip for anyone who feels they're being followed is to throw surprising blips into the daily grind. And if you are concerned that someone is on your tail, may have nefarious reasons for eyeballing you too long over a cup of coffee in the mall food court, go ahead and drop a little unpredictable turn in your route home. Duck into a gym like you're ready to take a spin on the stationary bike, then scan the parking lot for still shapes sitting and watching behind the wheel of a parked car, that kind of thing.

If you're feeling secure in your new day-to-day, adhering to a routine keeps you locked in your anonymous groove. No waves made means no flash flooding your new life.

What about roadblocks, though? I've already gamed a literal roadblock scene to gift you with a little taste of an issue you may have to confront as someone who has taken the non-societally approved move of adopting a new name, life, even persona, if possible.

The roadblocks encountered doing this, though, are obviously not all literal cops standing in the middle of a suburban side street ready to rob you of your freedom and donuts. Let's have a fun and eye-opening look at all the ways this could go bad for us!

Talking! Say you are in the final stages of getting out. Say you've got all the papers in place and now all you need to do is execute the exit strategy. Then say it occurs to you that you're pretty proud of what you've got set up. Seriously, some people—in spite of the fearful reasons that often prompt a move like this—might be tempted to brag. Maybe call up that one cousin, Timmy, who never truly believed in you, to impress him with this incredibly clever move. Your ego is your own worst roadblock. You're doomed to fail the moment some operator—be they cop or bad guy's henchman—comes to Timmy's door to casually inquire where that slugabed cousin of his might be. The cops will definitely go that far if you are facing charges, and the bad guys will, too.

They might even throw a little murder in for good measure. So then you'll have poor Timmy on your conscience and some cut-rate cutthroat on your tail.

Working! I've already touched on the perils of old routines and the pleasures of locking into new hobbies that have nothing to do with your old life. One related aspect of that is worth some focus here: jobs. Do not go back to doing whatever you did before.

If I could go back to what I was doing before, would I? Well, I put an awful lot of heart and soul into it—not to mention the years it took to acquire that law degree and shiny reputation. Ask yourself about what you've done that was an investment for you: medicine, education, animal husbandry—and think about how easy it would be to give that jalopy a jump-start and get it going again. No can do. If you've got the proper papers to fool an employer, get a job in another field entirely. Figure out something you could do as a general contractor, depending on your skills. Freelancers often need only fill out a tax form and some kind of quick-and-dirty contract for work. No need to rig a background check. Best-case scenario, you don't go back to work at all—but if you have to, try to find employment that leaves the sparsest paper trail.

Crime! If crime was how you made your money before you took off for the frontier, there may be a case for continuing down that path. If you were pretty good at it, that is. Though: how good could you be to end up here? This goes against the preceding advisory about doing a different job all together, but I understand that there's sometimes no comparable "straight" career to many of the fine and lucrative positions available to any up-and-coming drug dealer or enforcer out there.

If you're looking to get back into the game, remember to tread lightly. You're staring down a brand-new town of folks who are inclined not to trust fresh faces. A world of snitches, informants, and psychopaths who would shoot you with one hand while fondling a hoagie with the other. So if you were an enforcer, maybe try going somewhat "straight" by contracting with local bars to be a bouncer. If you made your dough by muling your drug of choice around, look into the life of a courier. There's a skill set beneath the skill set that made you good at the thing you used to do.

On the flip side, I'm not only thinking of criminals here, but of crime victims! What if you get mugged and robbed of all your new papers? Or lose access to your money? Immediately, you're thrust into a situation that would force just about anyone to instinctively seek assistance—but the closest you ever want to be to a cop is sharing a line at the Ponderosa. One tried-and-true thing I've said a million times holds true more now than ever before: should you encounter a crime while living under an assumed identity, *shut the hell up!* Do not talk to the cops. If worse turns worst, involve an attorney— they are bound by law to keep your secrets.

Driving! This will be tough for some, but driving any vehicle that requires a license after you've skipped out on your old life presents so many potential issues I'm not sure where to begin. I've mentioned one: the old-fashioned dragnet-style roadblock. A DUI checkpoint would be a near-identical situation. Cops are trained to carefully scrutinize all those papers you hand them at such a checkpoint. It won't matter if you're sober—I was about to say, "as a judge," then I remembered many of the judges I had the pleasure to meet in the courtroom— and have been teetotaling all your life. If Officer Mc-Muffin detects anything *off* in your papers, he or she will want to make their inspection a little more invasive. If your fake papers, cards, everything aren't perfect, your best bet may be to not drive at all. No car, no motorcycle, not even your big green tractor. Stick with rollerblades and riding lawnmowers to get around.

For the average American not living in a metropolitan hub, that will be a real downer, especially if you live in an area where commuter services are few and far between. The best solution really is to acquire a quality state ID, then use public transportation, walk, bike.

Even a nifty little scooter might do, if you don't find the prospect of putt-putting around town on one too embarrassing.

Of course, it's still possible to drive without a proper license. There are sovereign citizen types who will tell you that it's even constitutional under something called "right to travel." But good luck with that one if you get pulled over—if you're already living under a different name and have assumed a whole new life, the last thing you want is to get deep into any legal weeds regarding whether it's okay to be piloting whatever vehicle you have without an actual operator's license. Besides, people often apply the phrase "constitutional right" to a cornucopia of topics without reading the fine print on the sacred text—so buyer beware when it comes to that defense.

If you do drive without a license, make sure everything about your vehicle that might draw police attention is in perfect order. Tags look authentic and up-to-date; all lights functioning properly, tires in good shape. Follow all traffic laws to the letter—don't scoot an inch past the stop sign, be cautious turning right on red. After all, being a lousy driver was what ended up getting serial killer Ted Bundy arrested, in the end. We've gotta raise the bar above Ted Bundy, right?

Romancing! Far be it for me to discourage anyone from seeking companionship. Romantic attachments after you've adopted a new persona could end up being the biggest obstacle you face. Clark Rockefeller? Once he had a kid, his shriveled heart found a spark, and it ultimately led to him sitting in prison for the next few decades or so. Lori Ruff's life as Becky Sue then Lori Kennedy seemed to hum along just fine until she married and had children.

What's life without a warm candle to light up your night? The trick is: flames burn. I don't know about you, but I've seen people who were straight-out geniuses ultimately fail to keep major secrets from the ones they love. If you let that fire too close to the paper-thin walls of your new identity, it's all going to go up in smoke. And I know what you're thinking: love conquers all! He or she will accept my sins and stay by my side forever! Maybe. My pals in divorce court could spin you tales of outcomes so tragic that they'd make Cupid himself put down his bow and weep.

I'm not saying you have to spend the rest of your life a self-gratifying, sad hermit alone in the dark, of course not! Not unless that's your bag! But, the moment you start anything that looks like it might last, you should start preparing whomever you're seeing for the fact that you're an international man or woman of mystery.

No elaborate cover story, and for the sake of all the saints don't come up with some cockamamie explanation about being in the CIA. Actual spooks don't talk about it at all, not ever, and it's a big, neon-lettered invitation to others to be extremely curious about you. Curiosity is the killer, and you are the cat. Your past should be easily explained to a potential partner in under a minute: you're an orphan, from a place you don't like, with a past too painful to discuss.

Still, the safest bet may be casual dating. Keep your heart close, even when your aroused bits go hitch-hiking. The people who care about you will always put you in the most jeopardy, so whatever you do: don't do it lightly.

Living a Life of Boredom and Paranoia

Picture this: there's a full moon lighting the barren walls of your woodsy cottage. You've worked your way through *150 Ways to Play Solitaire*. Twice. As you flip over that last King, you might be struck by the profound thought: death is it. A life full of gripping paranoia and unwavering boredom, leading up to an anticlimactic final expiration.

As it turns out, staying low-profile, maintaining a steady schedule, and working a job so mind-numbing that it would put an anesthesiologist to sleep—it's not that interesting. And the paranoia? Who needs caffeine when you have an escalating series of poor choices to keep you up at night? Don't get me wrong, I'm not trying to discourage you. We're already too deep in to backtrack now, so let's see what we can do to encourage a bit of self-care:

With the boredom . . . it's an understandable human tendency to get a little cuckoo-bananas without mental stimulation. It's what makes solitary confinement so effective. It's what separates astronauts from the rest of us philistines.

If your life prior to disappearing was as action-packed as a Steven Seagal movie, let's be honest: it was probably pretty exhausting. But, it may have been the adrenaline rush that kept you going. Even if your life wasn't a page-turning thriller before, the life of a khaki-clad drone isn't for everyone. The intellectual withdrawal can start to grind at you.

There's no need to get morose yet! Examine this stuff in terms of a balance sheet. Make lists of pros and cons. There's a whole lot more in the plus column outweighing the cons of blowing your cover. Here's an example . . .

Pro: behaving in a routine way draws little attention from others. No one will notice if you wear the same pair of pants two days in a row, and you can eat all the salad you want without obsessively checking your teeth.

Con: if attention is your bread and butter, not getting any could really drag you down. You extroverts are going to suffer, there's no way around it. Hopefully we can find a way for you to cope with the lack of social stimulation that doesn't start with a "d" and end with an "issociative disorder."

Pro: Relinquishing a few of your social engagements will free up a sizable chunk of time for you to read all of the Great Books. I'm looking at you, *Ulysses*! Just say yes.

See? The boredom's not all bad.

What I'm really into right now, though, is the paranoid part of the festivities. By now it's got to be crystal clear to you that constant wariness is a necessary survival tactic. However, sometimes a logical paranoia can be overtaken by the slightly more unstable kind. The kind that tells you that you can't fall asleep because there's a monster in the closet shaped like an ICE agent with a really big Taser. That's when you can really get into trouble, because irrational paranoia lets fear take the wheel in a way that will seriously draw too much attention.

Healthy paranoia will keep you alive, but unhealthy

paranoia will land you on the front page or six feet underground.

Surveillance

There's surveillance—of an individual, a possible fugitive, a suspect, a mark, whatever—and then there's what I think of as Surveillance with a capital *S*. Call it Big Brother, Skynet, whatever: it's creepy as hell and unfortunately a very real fact of life today.

Truth is, global surveillance by big governments may be your biggest obstacle, especially if you're hotfooting it away from your old life because you're wanted for a crime. I don't assume everyone who hears or reads these words is a wanted fugitive, but reality is reality—that's often the exact reason a citizen chooses to vacate their former existence.

Saul, you may ask, is that a real thing? Well, yes. It's been pretty big news if you tune in to the six o'clock at all, how a whistle-blower or two let it be known that the American National Security Agency—aka the N.S.A.—has its digital tentacles wrapped around nearly every aspect of online life.

Of course, it might be easy to write that off as normal military behavior. If you're not a terrorist, for example—and I really hope you're not—then maybe you don't have to worry about the N.S.A. Or something like ECHELON. "Five Eyes." If you haven't heard of that tasty piece of dystopia, it's just a little system put in place by the biggest English-speaking countries around the world to track pretty much everyone. ECHELON's been denied, officially, but there have been plenty of huge whistle-blower leaks that proved it exists in some form. As they explain in a movie about one of those whistle-blowers, systems like ECHELON act like a typical search engine, only they can search whatever the hell they want and privacy can take a long walk off a short pier.

Besides, the fun part about surveillance is that it's available to snatch you up right here at home, wherever you are! I'll list a few homegrown forms of surveillance that can trip up anyone simply trying to live out their new life in peace.

Security Cameras. Friend, don't underestimate how insanely prevalent the lowly, passive security camera is nowadays. I've seen true crime shows based solely on reconstructing crime stories through the actual footage from those eyes-of-god mounted every ten feet on your average city block. You know: "here's the victim buying gas; here's the killer splashing gas on the victim; here's the match being lit," and so on. Even if you move to the most out-of-the-way locale you can think of, it would be a mistake to assume there aren't cameras lurking. There are amateur meteorologists living on cul-de-sacs who have weather cameras running 24/7. An inquisitive peace officer idly curious about some suspicious actions on your part might check for that at a neighbor's house and acquire footage of your daily comings and goings.

Passive surveillance is everywhere: gas stations, supermarkets, laser tag arenas . . . at this point, the list is endless. It's best to keep a pocketable disguise on hand in case you have to make like a tree and grab the first cab out of Dodge. If you're trying to live a quiet new life, it's a fine idea to have something on-hand anytime you're out running. Make it a game! Pretend you're a movie star avoiding the paparazzi. Only in your case, the shutterbugs might be wielding Tasers and warrants, or—even worse—an insatiable resentment over an unpaid debt and the machete to prove it.

Cell phone towers. One recommendation for someone who has dropped off the grid and changed their identity is to keep no cellular phone at all. That's tough, but not impossible. You'll find a way to live without customizable ringtones. If you can't survive without the option of dialing up Mr Moviefone and living vicariously through film listings, another option is to pick up the most basic, disposable "burner" phone you can find. The old-fashioned clamshell flip phone is still readily available at the finest bodegas, dusty convenience stores, and many other somewhat-sketchy authorized retailers. There's something to be said about smart phones being too "smart" for their own good. Those pocket NSA-receivers are constantly projecting metric tons of information about you, even when you're not making a call or checking your e-mail. Some of that you could fix, but that isn't common knowledge.

Most smart phones automatically embed the time, date, and *geographic location* into every photo you take. The geolocation is pretty easy to deactivate, but anyone casually analyzing an uploaded photo could still figure out a few things about you with that switched off. And cell phone towers are recording all the traffic that flows through their system, all the time—often including your approximate distance from the tower. Police have been known to track cell users from tower to tower, easily mapping a route from—in the case of a criminal—crime scene to hidey-hole. This is also true of burner phones, but at least you can swap them out frequently, and there's no "family plan" tying your temporary number to a permanent physical address.

StingRays. I love a good visit to the aquarium. The

soothing darkness, the playful sea otters, the gulping an-
chovies? But these StingRays aren't the kind you can
gently pet in the kiddie corner of your local marine center.

These StingRays track cell phones, but that's damn
sure not all they do. They can also function like a sub-
stitute cell phone tower for your little device to ping
away at to its delight. The cops can set one up, then access your phone's serial number, location, and more—
they can even block calls by disrupting the phone's ability
to connect to its service provider. The main thing you
need to know is that it's a tool the police use, and chances
are you've even had those invisible signals shooting out
of your phone go through one at some point. This technology is on the ACLU's radar, because these devices
sweep up information not just about their targets, but
also any innocent bystanders whose cell phones happen
to be within range of the police's trick tower.

The good news is StingRays are usually only deployed
if there's a concern about terrorism, civil unrest, or both.
Here are two simple tips to keep you out of the Sting-
Ray's barbed grasp: don't be a terrorist, and don't riot.
How hard is that? Just stay away from parades and
Black Friday sales. And good God, whatever you do, do
not be a rioting terrorist. That's a sure ticket to getting
busted in a big way.

Communication is still a necessity, even if it's just for

the most basic stuff. If modern electronic messaging of any kind is so at the mercy of ECHELONs and Sting-Rays, what choice do you have? I can't get too technical, but I can point you in the direction of some stuff that might get you where you want to go.

Know how I've been saying this is almost like being a spy? Here's where the overlap is obvious. So come on, Mr. or Ms. Bond, let's step into the shop where Q left his gear laying around and see what we can dig up to help you. Let's double back a little to the subject of . . .

PART III

The Internet

⚖

Never tweet! or snap, or pin, or whatever . . . It might be pretty outdated in a lot of ways now, but in the movie *Hackers* one character says, "You could sit at home, and do like absolutely nothing, and your name goes through like 17 computers a day. *1984*? Yeah right, man. That's a typo. Orwell is here now. He's livin' large."

That guy has a point and it's truer now than ever. Hey, I know this is a theme, but there's a gold-plated, indestructible reason it bobs back up again. Remember our case studies? The mystery dead guy on the Australian beach, Joey Newts, even Clark Rockefeller? None of them, not even the Clarkster, were in the same boat as you or me. See, unlike those mysterious characters, you and I are in an excellent position to have the Internet trip us right the hell into an 8×8 cell—even if you weren't fleeing the criminal justice system in the first place. This is the most connected, chatty age imaginable. The age of the tweet. The age of endless photo albums digitally preserved for all eternity on Facebook, where perhaps one day our great-grandkids can go to find our lives memorialized every bit as boring as they seem right now.

Sure, it's a glorious time! Gigantic databases of information everywhere, linked by glowing fiber-optic cables speeding information along at incredible speeds! Anything you need, at your fingertips. Give me my flying car and my robot maid, I'm all ready for this *Jetsons* kind of life.

Oh, no, wait—that all comes at a very steep price. If you want access to everything, you must allow yourself to be accessible, too. Anyone who has dropped off the grid and wants to stay gone has to take a very different tack when it comes to the Internet.

The idea of not using the Web at all is kind of weird. It also could conceivably set up an unfortunate attention-grabbing situation, where casual work acquaintances or neighbors figure out that woman in 3-A doesn't seem to exist online, which sets off alarm bells. It's okay to be a Luddite, as long as you're believably Google-able.

We've chatted about how it's mandatory that your old online life goes as dead as the poor soul whose social security number you're currently using. That's a given.

But say you need to have some kind of basic online presence, because even the most minimal lease agreement nowadays might have a line for "e-mail address." It's become one of those things people just automatically include on forms, presumably because no one likes to talk on the phone anymore.

Also, the Internet will remain incredibly valuable to you if you want to keep tabs on what's going on with your old life. Not that you should! It's safer to stay away, but supposing you glance through the online version of your local paper from time to time, there's probably no harm—just don't comment on any news stories. I don't care if Mrs. Sarah Sabatini is claiming to have baked the most delicious pecan pie eight years in a row and you know it to be a fact that you held the blue ribbon at least twice in that range—bite your tongue, bite your fingertips, and close the page.

This all presents a problem, though, and that problem is spelled IP, or Internet Protocol Address. Every computer has an IP address, and it's a string of digits that might look like this: 110.55.106.175 (that one's fake). Depending on what Internet service you use—and several other factors—an IP can be traced right down to your front door.

I am not kidding. A killer in St. Louis once tried to taunt cops with an Internet map of the location of a victim's body. The police ended up finding his IP and that led them straight to his Microsoft screen name. That bland-looking string of numbers can cause a whole world of hurt, the kind of hurt you can only plea-bargain down to an ankle bracelet, and that's if you're lucky.

Never fear, though! In this instance, the feared hackers of today have found creative ways to sidestep the Orwellian surveillance they were already onto when the movie *Hackers* came out.

If I've already spooked you enough about using the Internet, consider doing the following research from some kind of common-use public computer. Those can be found in various hotel lobbies (though they may require a guest password) and libraries, or used for a small sum at print shops like Kinkos. I'd elbow the covert masturbators out of the way and opt for the library, but your mileage may vary.

Onionize Your Online Life. I don't even claim to understand how it works, but over the years, Internet geniuses have put together something called Tor, which stands for The Onion Router. What Tor actually does for you is dirt-simple and might be a relief to the nervous guy or gal on the run from a heap of troubles at home. Tor is free, downloadable software that that allows anyone who has it on their computer to do their work in complete and blessed anonymity. As best as I can understand, Tor's network routes signals all over the world, until an Internet user's identification and location have been completely obscured.

An argument in favor of getting your hands dirty with technical stuff and using Tor is pretty simple: criminals are really fond of it. All along I've assumed I'm talking to a mix of people—those fleeing legal woes and those who are just trying to get away from some kind of clear and present danger, which often involves terrible people (abusive spouses, creepy stalkers, people who compulsively suck their teeth in restaurants). Any of these would be well served by a software package that's popular with online drug merchants, sellers of questionable documents (also relevant to our cause here!), and hackers themselves.

I've been told that Tor, sadly, isn't perfect. Law enforcement and government agencies have learned in the last few years that if they park themselves at key points along Tor's network, they may be able to identify some users.

However, knowing the way criminal justice enforcers prioritize what they do, I can almost guarantee that unless you are one seriously bad actor and your Internet habits are part of whatever files exist about you, chances are good they won't have their bots hanging out looking for signs of you trying to anonymously purchase your favorite vintage train conductor overalls on eBay.

I began by instructing you, grasshopper: don't tweet. I was serious about that. Listen, get your anonymity software. Set up a basic e-mail account that only receives, never sends. Go absolutely crazy with searching whatever you need to search to reassure yourself that whoever might be a little too curious about you is not actually on your trail, yet.

But let's look at the temptation, the real snake in the garden of your new life free of old and possibly deadly entanglements. Temptation comes in the form of whatever social media venue tickles your attention-seeking fancy. If you are involved with social media when you realize it's time to hightail it out of your old life, then I have some ugly reality for you: your new life needs to be about staying the hell off those accounts.

Why? Because we're humans, and we are creatures of habit. I'm not just talking about consistently lusting for spicy mustard on our hot dogs, I'm talking about speech patterns. The way we actually construct sentences.

If you had a really popular social media account of some kind prior to bugging out and you did as instructed and let that drop, great. What you don't want to give into is the impulse to start up something similar all over again, a lonely nobody this time, of course, but with the same unmistakable verbal flair. The Internet is full of intrepid amateur detectives who are spending their free time catching "catfish" and surfing the profiles of innocuous strangers.

Depending on how hard someone is searching for you, even your tendency to use the words "cromulent" and "perq" in casual conversation might trip you up. If you're a highly prized fugitive for some reason—major bank robbery suspect, drug trafficker, and the like—federal investigators have a pretty deep bag of tricks to reach into, and it's not crazy to think they could find you simply by analyzing anything you've posted on the Internet and then using tailored search strings to discover that mysterious nobody in Podunk, Idaho, who— wow, crazy coincidence—*looks just like you.*

The bottom line is this: keep the Internet shenanigans to the barest minimum possible. And when you have to do anything—it's highly likely you still may have to conduct various financial activities over a computer, for example—hide behind whatever walls you can find. An unmonitored public computer you can type on with gloved hands, the Tor-obscured surfing software, whatever works.

It's not all about computers and tablets though, is it? At some point, we have to talk to people. That's a fact of life. So let's go to church together, my friends. I'm about to induct you into . . .

The Blessed Cult of the Burner Phone

I know that if you've been an avid consumer of detective novels, thrillers, cop dramas, you've heard of the burner phone. Just what the hell is a burner phone, after all, and is it even a real thing? Do you set it on fire after you use it? It's real, and it could be your best friend. And you are not required to set it ablaze, no.

On a simple level, a burner phone is a prepaid cell purchased with cold, hard cash. No contract to worry about. You pick up some airtime cards (like what you'd buy to use a pay phone overseas), maybe $50 for a month, whatever the going rate is now, charge up the phone, and then use it for whatever.

It's not fiction that our friends who society so judgmentally condemns as "the criminal element" are longtime users of burner phones. I have to admit, too, they are much more convenient than driving out to the last working pay phone wherever you live, if there even is an operable one anymore.

So, you've got a solid source of communication and even the cheapest phone probably has some basic ability to use the Internet—and then when you think the number may have run through one too many StingRay devices, just drop it in the trash as you're exiting your local big box store with the box containing your next burner phone.

Of course, it's wrong to assume a burner phone is only of use to those who want to keep phone calls related to their drug deals off their AT&T bill. The burner phone has completely—well, mostly—legitimate uses as well.

Acquiring funds is a continuing challenge, especially if the money you piled up to finance your life change was more molehill than mountain. It seems inevitable that before you can find some basic job in your new life, you might need to downsize. A pretty natural way of doing that these days might be some kind of anonymous ad on a Web site that specializes in classified postings.

What could be safer for something like that than a completely disposable phone number? Hell, you could put it right in the ad, in that case. Then once you've sold that pair of ski boots and the transaction is done, the phone number can conveniently flutter off to the dead phone number graveyard and your new pal won't be able to invite you to tag along on any wintry adventures. Not to mention, no further hassles from the nosy, weird, or disgruntled buyers who found your posting a little too late.

Burner phones are incredibly useful to anyone on the dating scene, too. What better option to have at your disposal than a disposable phone if your new flame gets a little stalkerish? What if they suddenly realize you aren't actually Kevin Costner or Jennifer Aniston's hotter older sister? Flip that phone open and snap it right down the middle—there will no longer be a place for your suitor to file a complaint, and everyone can move on with their lives.

Burners are eminently practical solutions to a ton of problems. Coming back to how they might be relevant to our interests—well, you need to have some kind of phone number when applying for your low-key job in your new life, right? That's a business application, in a way. Also, if you're among that "criminal element" I mentioned before, you don't really need me explaining burner benefits to you.

Buying the burner phone is a pretty simple affair. Some of those phones are so inexpensive now that casually dropping one in the trash doesn't even feel like you're throwing money away. There's a catch here, though—some states legislators are getting wise to the burner phenomenon and beginning to put legislation in place that might require an ID even for your economical $9.99 clamshell. Hey, that's fine if you have your well-made fake ID or a valid state card with your new name and address on it—except it still feels like an extra layer of information tracking that you might not want to deal with in your new life.

So is there another option, aside from burners? The answer is a measured "yes."

Maybe you can acquire a single phone and stick with it, if you use other evasive measures.

I've had *67 recommended to me. Dial those digits prior to whatever number you're calling, and your number and identification will be blocked from whoever's on the other end. Problem with *67 is that it's not too reliable. In a worldwide communications system that's subject to some giant spying octopus monster like ECHELON, *67 feels a little too simple. Other keystrokes may do the same thing—I believe *31 is an option on some cells—but it doesn't feel much more solid.

If you're going ahead and using one of the major kinds of smart phone, there is an app available that can churn out a burner number for you to use as long as you like. That's great for making calls to find out information about whether your "disappearance" is under investigation, for calling and spooking old enemies, or making random threats (which I would not recommend, but the heart wants). However, it doesn't change the problem of that smart phone gathering a ton of other data even while you're happily harassing folks under the burner app cover.

A good strategy for the burner phone, then: buy it well before you make your exit. Keep it simple, go with the old-fashioned non-smart phone. Set it up with your new name or as "anonymous," whichever you're allowed to do. Keep it charged and ready to go. Hell, they're so cheap—buy three and take them all with you. The more the merrier. Think of the burner phones as a kind of insurance policy against a host of troubles often encountered by brave travelers like you.

Oh, the Empty Places You'll Go!

It sounds like the title of the grimest children's book ever, but we're all big kids here, I'm guessing. So let's really dive into the pressing issue of where to go to hopefully even stay, once you're ready.

Location, location, location! In all kinds of real estate, it's the most vital thing. When you've dropped off the grid, assumed a new identity and hopefully begun a brand new life in earnest, location becomes about ten times more important than it's ever been before.

It may surprise you how many choices you have. . . .

City Living

Your options aren't just a tent in the woods or a lonely shack outside a prairie town! Giant megacities are an option. I know of a guy who peaced out on his U.S. Army commitments, even though the military is not an at-will employer. They will happily hunt you down for saying sayonara to Uncle Sam without going through the proper channels. This guy managed, however, to go to ground in New York City, the City that Never Sleeps, and he did it for two full years before electing to turn himself in and face the consequences—for his own reasons. In NYC, our buddy managed to hold a job and blend in with the bustling crowd, and he could have easily kept that up for many more years.

Big cities, then, are absolutely an option for wherever you want to go next. They offer great commuter services, which you can ride anonymously all day long. Many landlords in a big city's less fortunate neighborhoods are also exceedingly generous about renting to just about anyone who can pony up the money for the first and last month's rent plus a security deposit. That is, you'll get the place just as long as you're not doing the walk-through while chewing on actual human body parts. But that's the drawback, too—neighborhoods like that, your chances of becoming a crime victim go way up, and your inability to remedy that because you're laying low remains the same.

Not to mention, there are cameras on every street corner and in every single electronics shop and chic cold brew coffee café on every block of a modern metropolis. The surveillance state is a real thing. No, that fearsome future world of all cameras being linked and checking your mug against some database isn't quite here yet, but it's close. And let's say any kind of investigator looking for you—skip tracers, private detectives, cops—gets a whiff of your general location. One of those men or women gets the idea that your new routine has you bumbling down Main Street each day in search of coffee, it's a sure bet they will start figuring out how to get hold of whatever video surveillance footage there may be along the way. Who wouldn't? And if that footage is introduced to the right video analysis software, there's an outside chance even your new Groucho glasses and White Sox ball cap will not shield you from the camera's all-seeing gaze.

Big cities also present more opportunities to run into cops on the regular, which may be hazardous to both the career criminal and the innocent on the run from a bad situation. For one, the chance encounter with an inquisitive peace officer who has a better than average memory for faces on BOLO sheets could kill a newfound life of freedom fast. For the other, there's the whole predicament of missing persons flyers—always distributed at police stations—as well as posters shared online.

I'm just ticking off a few of the disadvantages that come with trying to lose yourself inside a bustling big city. There are many more.

But then there's the flip side of the coin.

Hobo Living!

This one is really not my cup of whatever's good, hot, and tasty, but as I've said before, it's a valid option. Remember talking about the emergency hobo bug-out and how to have some baseline plan in place to get there? That was fun, but I haven't fully covered the issue of actually *living* as a wayfaring stranger the rest of your days.

Advantage numero uno, and this is a biggie: it's about as off-the-grid as you can get. Roaming from town to town, riding the rails even (yes, still totally possible in many parts of the country), camping out in nature and communing with the stars in the fresh, open air. However, you'd also be communing with wild animals, anti-vagrancy laws, and other hobos, who may or may not be into killing fellow hobos for sport. Maybe that's an urban legend, but it's a pervasive one that should haunt your dreams!

Look, if you really are down with this option, I'm going to say you need to be on the younger side of things and in decent physical shape before you even begin. Men and women stand about an equal chance of getting killed during an ill-advised hop from the caboose of a northbound freight train out of Las Cruces.

Intentionally going full nomad is a different ball of wax than slipping out of your former life and reestablishing a new homestead elsewhere. Money is different—I'd argue you that you need more cash to start with and a really good way to hide it—and you'll also want to plan some kind of route before you get moving.

Nice thing about that is if you are down with natural living, the United States of America already has a long and winding path laid down for you, and if you play your cards right, there is every chance you could live along this path and never run into unwanted prying eyes again. Other people, sure, but not detectives either private or government-paid. They rarely strap on the hiking boots when they're on duty. I'd add: some of these natural solutions to disappearing and rebooting your life may not be great for more than a kind of buffering strategy, but they're a way to give yourself time to think the next steps through. . . .

The Appalachian Trail

Me? Well, I'm honestly more of a city guy. I can't help it if I'm a fan of the readily available goods and services that exist in even the most out-of-the-way municipalities. But *if* I lost my mind completely and elected to take the hobo option, I'll tell you one place I might go: East, young friend. I would cross the mighty Mississippi River, and shuffle on into Old Dixie and eventually make my way to the southern head of the roughly 2,200 mile Appalachian Trail.

The trail's southern end begins in Georgia and it ends in Maine. If you look at it on a big map of America, it looks like a slightly squiggly but semi-straight line running up the country.

Before you reject the idea out of hand as equivalent to an attempted mounting of Everest, consider this:

chances are, you wouldn't be the only lonely soul out on that trail hiding from life, the universe, or a Juarez-based assassin nicknamed The Grapefruit. A quick case study is worth mentioning when it comes to defending the trail option.

We'll just use his first name, James. He had a fine job handling vendor accounting and payments for his firm in one of Ohio's big cities. Then one day, James— a well-respected and veteran employee—was called in regarding evidence of fraud afoot within the company. James told those federal investigators he didn't know squat. He left work, returned to his home in Kentucky, and promptly disappeared.

Cut to roughly five years down the road.

An Appalachian Trail enthusiast was sitting at home watching TV, a true crime show that sometimes profiled fugitives on the run. The show aired a segment about a guy wanted by the FBI for embezzling a cool $8.7 million from his Ohio employer over the course of eleven years or so. I don't know what said trail-lover thought at the time, but it was probably something on the order of "Holy shitwhistles," because there on the flat screen the hiker saw the face of a trail buddy known only as "Bismarck."

Bismarck was not some displaced German royal, he

was James from Ohio! The guy had disappeared after the FBI interrogation, packed up whatever he needed, and proceeded to spend the next several years, in the FBI's own words, "hiding in plain sight on the Appalachian Trail."

Right away you probably see, after all we've discussed here, where our pal went wrong: he was a friendly, outgoing sort, and easily made pals along the trail.

Still, we're not here to condemn James, but to praise him. Were it not for his unfortunate extroversion, he might still be making his way up and down that immense trail today. He chose well, too. The Appalachian Trail has a few dangers, but if you're going to vanish into any kind of wilderness, it also has major advantages.

It's well-marked, to the degree that you kind of have to work at getting lost. There are shelters along the trail and plenty of campsites. If you have gone at least as far as a fake ID, then there are plenty of homes, cabins, you name it along parts of the trail. Their owners and landlords are happy to help campers out with shelter sometimes.

Considering its length, the Appalachian Trail isn't really all *that* dangerous. There have been violent crimes, but they're pretty rare—as are predators from the animal kingdom. As a hiker goes north into New England, the biggest threat is going to be the frigid winter. If you use trail guides and pay attention to the passing of the seasons, you could end up hiding out just like Bismarck Jim—maybe longer if you're careful about concealing your appearance when dealing with others. Even better: try to avoid them all together!

If this has you excited at the prospect of life in the great wide open, hey, that's wonderful. Grow your Grizzly Adams beard right now, put your hair in a pioneer woman's braid, and start prepping your mess kit.

However, if this is a full-lifetime life change you're looking at, confront the prospect of trying to grow old out there. The Appalachian Trail might be, at best, a short-term solution. But if you have the time to put together a decent bug-out bag and you've been blessed with some camping knowhow from an outdoorsy friend or a long run with the Scouts, it seems like the perfect solution to give you time to think about your next move.

By the way, finding a way to Georgia and starting there is not your only option. There's the American Discovery Trail, which cuts across the center of the nation; a trail along the Continental Divide in the west; and the Pacific Crest Trail, which runs the length of the West Coast. Any of them will provide a scenic path to appreciate for a while, at least until some of the heat is off.

Disappearing into the Desert

This might seem like a part of some kind of outdoorsy theme I've got going on, but it's not. I'm talking about a camouflaging move, a fake-out.

There is no better place to vanish than the desert. Think about the environment: no one wants go wandering through that bone-dry wasteland. Trust me when I say you don't willingly head out into the desert unless there's an urgent need for privacy and/or someone has you at gunpoint.

No one wants to follow you into the desert. It's just creosote bushes, tarantulas, death, and eventual mummification awaiting you out there.

If you bring enough water and find some shade, sure— you can disappear, but only as a stopgap measure. Step one on the road to becoming your new self—at least that's how I look at it. Plenty of folks live out in the desert. They make their homes there. The oh-so-generous U.S. government many years ago graciously bequeathed our native brethren huge sections of desert for reservations (that's sarcasm, for those who have trouble discerning tone).

If there's a desert within driving distance of where you are, there's value in using it to convince anyone who might be on your tail that following you could be fruit-less. Someone wants you dead, and you head straight for a barren hellscape? They're going to assume you're doing their job for them.

Consider a few different gambits in the desert wan-derer game as a way to convince those who knew you in your old life that you're gone for good.

Suicide. A casual stroll into the dry lands in just about any season with no apparent return path is a sure way to buy the farm beside a cactus. If you're looking to disappear forever in the eyes of the lawmen or at mini-mum the ex-husbands seeking you, concoct an apparent desert suicide. This would involve some serious plan-ning and careful attention to blurring your trail, but it isn't impossible. Follow one of the many unpaved roads that lead from state highways through desert lands. Park your car next to an ND vehicle that you just happened to drop off there at an earlier point in time. For good mea-sure, leave a door open and a plaintive note about your tortured existence here on this physical plane. Trudge a certain distance, then trudge a little farther.

Turn around and head back, using a broom to brush away your returning tracks the rest of the way. Jump in the super-cheap secondary vehicle you purchased under a transitional or even your new assumed name, and drive off to freedom. The desert will tell the rest of the story, and folks will assume you've given your body to the wind and the sand. Hate to sadden people who cared like that, but it's a pretty good way to throw up a smoke screen without actually lighting anything on fire.

Homicide. This might be tough to fake without an accomplice, but it isn't impossible. The biggest problem is it might involve the homicide of another. Or at minimum, handling a dead body, which isn't pleasant for anyone but the one-legged groundskeeper at your local cemetery. He always seemed a little too cheerful.

There was this guy, a military dude whom we'll call Art. In the early 1990s, he was suspected of being incredibly creepy with the daughters of some of his colleagues-in-arms. Guys who are cretins around kids are the lowest of the low, so Art realized he could be in for a heap of trouble.

He settled on what was, despite his creepiness, a clever solution. He decided to die. Sort of. A charred skeleton was found in his burned-out trailer in the Nevada desert and the military wiped its hands and said, "well, that's that—here are his post-death benefits" to his dependents. The burned bones were interred in a military grave.

Art's plan unraveled a few years later when his daughters finally complained about him being incredibly creepy with them, too.

He'd used the desert as part of his cover, though, and for a while it worked. All that said, I still wouldn't recommend this particular solution to whatever problems you're facing. To put an edge keen enough to draw blood on this point o' mine: not a big fan of the desert, but it does have its uses. Be wary and careful.

Whatever you do, don't actually get stuck out there. At night it gets bitterly cold; during the day the sun and the windblown sand will race to burn the skin right off your face. If you're in a high-desert climate like what New Mexico has, the altitude might make you so dizzy that you forget to hydrate—and it's between you and your desiccated corpse to figure out what might go wrong if you find yourself dehydrated in the desert.

Moving right along to another climate . . .

Snowshoe Prints to Nowhere (or Canada)

A huge portion of the border between the United States and Canada is a long, straight line. Every few years crews descend from the Great White North and travel up from the American Midwest to mow and prune that strip of land. They cut trees, clear brush, make sure the little pylons buried in the ground that say "International

Border" are legible. Then they have celebratory beers and poutine, and go home.

Since 9/11/2001, that border—once the most casual of dividing lines between two friendly and fun-loving countries—has been a lot less porous than it once was. Still, the general affection that persists between Canada and the United States can't be completely crushed. That 49th parallel has a ton of heavily guarded and gated border crossings, sure, but it also has a number of areas where at first glance, it looks like damn near nothing is going on.

Let's dig into those parts of the border a little bit. I know I've confined a lot of talk about slipping out of an old life and into a new to the lower 48, but this is a good moment to address the possibility of slipping off to join our strapping, trapping friends in the North. If you're not on American soil as you read this, don't assume it might apply to some international border relevant to you, by the way. In some nations, every single inch of the borders are under scrutiny—in others, you can still gallivant across as if you own the world. Just keep up on current events, and you should have a good idea which of your neighbors might be most likely to take a siesta when looking in the direction of your home country.

Big buyer beware on this section: your humble host

here hasn't tried this personally, so take this research
with a big old grain of Pink Himalayan Salt.

The Art of Going Everywhere

Even people who bust out of their old lives and leave it
all behind for perfectly legit reasons like saving themselves from cutthroat psychopaths are still going to lengths
others might find kind of objectionable. If those in question have an extended family—moms, dads, siblings—
those relatives will probably think the gone girl or guy is
deceased. If said family finds out otherwise, they might
get pretty pissed at the deception.

My take on what to do in this situation is pretty
simple and it builds on things we've already talked about.
Remember the bug-out bag? Adopting a new name
and lifestyle, even altering your appearance, just doesn't
buy you an ironclad guarantee to a peaceful life from
here on out. You shouldn't expect a "clean slate" so much
as a slate that you shit all over and then ran through a
broken dishwasher, so it's still kinda streaky, but you
have to eat off it during every meal for the rest of your
life and hope that none of the toxic residue of your old
life mixes with this evening's Hamburger Helper.

Let me give you a scenario: say you took on a new

identity and exited the grid because your life was in danger from a group of people who think you're responsible for setting loose all the Thoroughbreds from their stables. It seemed suspicious to you that Old MacDonald happened to own the nearby glue farm, but now a band of farmers have come at you with pitchforks blazing, so you've got to find a home far away from the range. With assistance or by yourself, you put together a pretty neat setup, right down to a decent but nondescript job at an ice-cream parlor.

One day at work you see a guy who, based on his demeanor and denim overalls, seems like he might be the kind of dude the people looking for you would send out to do the job. Brawny, serious, tanned only to his T-shirt sleeves. A walking advertisement for FarmersOnly .Com. As he heads your way: your back stiffens, your pulse races, and a vanilla cone slips right through your trembling fingers. Just as the panic threatens to swallow you up—

—he passes right on by, intent on greeting a fellow patron who happened to be looking for a delicious afternoon treat. Still, what if he hadn't been? When you got off work that night and parked yourself in a spot where you could observe the front of your house for signs of entry—would you have a way out if you did spot someone sketchy?

That song by The Who says "don't get fooled again," but Saul says don't give 'em a chance to fool you the first time. If you smell smoke, don't bother to search for a fire extinguisher—stop, drop, and grab your prepacked bug-out bag.

Everywhere You Go, There You Are. Go-bags aren't the only safety protocols that you should have at the ready.

Some things are basic. If you are still in reasonably good physical shape—that is, you're capable of moving on your own two feet for at least five to ten minutes at a time, invest in some practical clothing ideal for the fugitive man or woman about town who might need to move fast at a moments' notice. Pack layers. Ditch the skinny jeans for trousers with deep pockets. Have solid, comfortable shoes ready to slip on—shoes you can run in, if need be. There's a company in Massachusetts making high-performance suits and shoes that you could run a marathon in. Science is on our side, here!

Think about the huge advantage of something like that. Perhaps you're a guy and you've found a job in the upstanding, low-stress field of insurance brokering. You've got to look sharp, so you purchase some suit separates that are advertised as being for the active male. Shoes, too. Then, the moment you get a whiff of a "client" who may be looking for something more than a decent premium, you can take off sprinting in the other direction. The average suit is not made for that. You could die of dehydration sweating inside a summer woolen. Even if you can't track down a space-age activewear suit, it can't hurt to at least keep a pair of sneakers in your trunk.

Better Call the Gym. Totally joking about the gym, my friend. If anything, my advice is to avoid having something like a gym membership in your new life. Avoid it like the plague. That's just another set of papers filled out in your handwriting and another set of surveillance cameras catching your sweaty face as you flop around on the treadmill. The serious part is this, though: it's a good idea to keep fit in the comfort of your own home. You've got to remain agile, mobile, ready to move whenever possible. So do a set of push-ups and some squats each morning, maybe some sit-ups every night, too—and you'll probably be good to go.

If nothing else, walking will do you a lot of good. No license or even ID is required, it gets you where you're going, and you stay in shape. When the grim reaper might be around the corner in the form of a newly unincarcerated enforcer with the nickname Kiddie Hitler, all that truly matters is you remain nimble enough to stay a few steps ahead.

Next up is a pretty important stopgap measure. The move that might keep a solid firewall between you and whomever is still a little too curious about your whereabouts after you've slipped off the radar. Let's talk mail drops, redirects, and other spycraft.

No Permanent, Fixed Address

Put down your bindle, this isn't more harping on the transitory glory of the hobo life.

Even though I've probably mentioned mail at least once already, we haven't really explored the world of obscuring yourself from the United States Postal Service and various other private but similar entities, like UPS and FedEx. This is an integral part of our plan to wipe you off the grid. Why? Because advertisers possess the ability to leverage details about your online purchases, real-world buying habits, and what Web site links you just happen to click on in order to track you down and keep marketing directly to you—and they're not the only ones with programmers hacking away night and day at formulas aiming to profile each and every one of us.

I don't mean that you shouldn't use the mail. If you are settling into a new life and living in an apartment, a house, even a well-built yurt, then chances are you will need to send and receive actual mail. In spite of the rallying cry to "go green" and folks predicting on an annual basis that traditional mail is dying: it ain't.

What about a good ol' post office box? A separation of church and physical address? Just as with the United States–Canada border crossings, a certain terrible date in recent American history made the easily rented post office box a thing of the past. Thanks to the Patriot Act, every U.S. Post Office box requires IDs, signatures, and the promise of some pretty ugly penalties for anyone who provides false information on the application forms. But what's more American than taking a few liberties? But if you're nervous about giving the Inspector General the slip, here are some alternate methods of communication . . .

The Anonymous Drop. Sounds like the name of a band that specializes in songs about computer hacking and *Star Trek* fan orgies, but no. An anonymous mail drop is a real thing and we've already mentioned one in passing, back when I told you about the mysterious Lori Ruff.

It might sound like it works in a pretty straightforward way. Anonymous mail drops receive mail intended for you at an address separate from your actual residence. The mail either stays at that place until you make a pickup or a third party sends it to wherever you actually are.

You can find one of these services pretty quickly online and set up an account—but there's a catch. Frequently, if you want mail that's coming from the U.S. Postal Service, a re-mailing service will need you to fill out one of the USPS's special forms that requires identification and notarizing (exactly the kind of trace you're looking to keep off the paper).

If your fake ID is solid and there's a way to finagle a notarization from a source you trust to turn a blind eye, great! But if you've come this far, I've taught you nothing if that doesn't set off a few red flags.

Okay, if the mail or parcels you expect are coming from a private service (UPS, DHL, whatever you use to TCB), you'll still be good with one of these standard-issue re-mailing services. But what about that U.S. mail hiccup?

Early in my storied career as one of the finest legal minds to ever grace a New Mexico courtroom, I had a modest office in the rear of another establishment. It was inexpensive and versatile, and the arrangement worked like gangbusters for everyone involved.

Across the country, in cities big and small, there are millions of strip malls, small office parks, and office buildings teeming with empty spaces identical to that office of mine in need of key-turning proprietors. Outside of expensive cities like San Francisco and New York, these places tend to run relatively cheap.

When you start casting around to set up your mail drop, do a little surveillance.

Let's assume you're going to settle down and make like a normal human, just with a new name and history, and you're doing it in a decent suburban or even urban area. Start looking for office buildings or parks that look a little long in the tooth. The landscaping has gone shaggy or the plaster has started to fall away. You find a workspace that could use a new coat of paint to cover a multitude of brown patches currently staining the ceiling? Welcome to your dream castle.

Next: find the rental office for that place. Tell the owner your business works out of home, but you really need a separate space to catch all your parcels. Not just regular mail, but FedEx and the like. Depending on how keen that owner or landlord is to have someone paying something more than zero dollars to keep the space occupied, you may be able to secure a mail drop to your new name for a firm handshake and $100 per month.

There are several variations of this kind of drop. Worldly traveler you are, you could befriend the owners of a small independently operated bed-and-breakfast. With the promise of your patronage each time you're traversing the near portion of the Appalachian Trail (or whatever granola-chewing endurance artists try to conquer in your area), you might be able to arrange to have mail sent to your new name at their address.

If you've been smooth enough over time with establishing your new life, then you could even get away with having mail sent to your new name at whatever address you currently reside.

However: remember the Spooky Magic of the Internet Algorithm? I'm talking about the way shopping and search habits can lead to a retailer knowing more about you than your boy- or girlfriend might.

If, under your new name and in your new life, you still like to shop at Big Box Mart and at some point you've relaxed enough into the new groove that you've given them your mailing address while purchasing a video game, who's to say it won't be used against you? More than one teen girl has found herself idly searching for baby items on one store's Web site and blam! a few weeks later, coupons for pregnancy-related items arrive at the home she shares with her folks—who definitely did not know she was pregnant. What better way to break the news than with a two-for-one deal on sun-proof baby bonnets?

I'm just trying to give you some idea of what you're

facing in a world where technology tightens its strangle-hold on our mortal existence every day.

Which, hey, if strangling is your thing, who am I to judge? If life hasn't thrown challenges, obstacles, hit men carrying hammers into your path, then all that inter-connectivity is not going to feel like such a big deal. But if you're among the unlucky who have discovered a real need to relocate, then some retail giant's computer algo-rithms profiling you via your love of movies starring Ray Milland may one day prove troublesome.

There are out-of-the-big-box solutions for everything, though. This one comes with a buyer beware: you prob-ably need to have the means to buy stuff to do it. I'm not saying you need to have a few million vacuum-sealed and stuffed in a climate-controlled storage facility. Maybe just the cash payout from selling your modest suburban home, say $150–$200,000. That might be enough to pur-chase an RV.

On the Road Again

We've all been driving down the highway, rocking out to the Artist Currently Known as Prince on the stereo, only to see one of those giant recreational vehicles cruising down the pavement ahead. And the general consensus reaction, without fail, is usually fear. After all, the soul behind the wheel of that slickly paneled road whale is probably old enough to make you wonder how she got the day pass from the elder home, much less access to a vehicle that rivals some semitrailers in size.

The fascinating thing about RVs is that some folks, old and young, manage to live year-round in the things. These nomads simply navigate campground to campground. North in the summer, south in the winter. Rent a site, maybe even hook up temporary water and electricity.

It's a little bit of a digression, but it occurred to me: is there any solution that might involve dropping out of sight without completely ditching all the other stuff? A slightly less complicated thing? Sure there is. There are plenty.

RV living is one solution. It's best for people who are not running away from a crime, whether as culprit or crime victim.

There have been cases where someone who wasn't a fugitive or in fear of another slipped off the grid. I can think of a couple of guys who lived with fake IDs, had apartments full of enough guns to arm a small militia, and seemed like generally secretive, sketchy dudes. Eventually they fell afoul of the law. Cops dug into their backgrounds expecting a trail of murder and mayhem, only to find . . . not much. Traffic tickets, maybe. These dudes were simply paranoid, and they didn't want to live an easily identifiable life.

This is just a little side road to acknowledge that some people don't exactly have anything to run from, but they still want to go. Fine. Sell the house, buy that giant van, and hit the road.

With the advantage of not needing to hide from the law, you have all the legit papers you need. A post office drop is no problem for you. You and your partner, if you have one, can plan an unpredictable crisscross of the country. If you're clean enough to have a passport, you can even thumb your nose at international borders, too, all while driving your own damned home around and keeping watchful eyes guessing at your next move.

It doesn't even require an RV—the more modestly endowed (financially speaking) could manage with one of those sharp-looking Sprinter vans. The kind with space-age tinted glass and high ceilings. You could cruise around the country in a swanky Mercedes, albeit a passenger van that can hold somewhere from twelve passengers to your entire mobile life.

I'm half-kidding, but as I touched on when we began, actually leaving the grid—which is way more of a frustrating funnel-style spiderweb—is only for the truly committed. To be that into the idea, the motivation has to be much stronger than merely getting tired of staying rooted to one place.

Unless the wolves are at the door or the creditor's hired repo predators are just around the corner, don't bother with all the dead kid birth certificate shenanigans, or with hiring some operator who can perfectly fake this stuff. Just buy a spacious vehicle and head out on the highway with your heavy metal thundering self.

Gaps

Plans can be laid as carefully as precisely cut stones meant to fit together without cement. Ducks in a perfect row, exact increments between their sizes from the big mama duck down to the tiniest duckling. A scheme plotted out on paper with mathematical precision, however, is still going to end up with some gaps between checkpoints.

If you've gotten this far and are still serious about dumping your old life down the drain like expired milk so that you can revamp and re-up for a few more decades under the radar, it might be a good idea to examine your plans for warps, woofs, and total calamities. There will be one or more of all these.

I've been steady all along with pointing out the rainbow of reasons your whole scheme might end up blown to smithereens, with you either in jail, dead, or wishing you were so lucky to be either. Let's zero in on that.

This Is How It Ends

There are many paths to absolutely screwing over a new life endeavor. One fun one to mention again, in case it wasn't clear every other time I jumped up and down on the point: talking. Loosening your lips for anyone is a big no-no, even if he or she is your soul mate, confidante, or co-consul of the secret ministry of secret administering.

> **YOU:** Granny, I'm gonna go away, just wanted to say good-bye.
> **GRANNY:** Oh no, where are you going?
> **YOU:** Now don't tell anyone, but I'm faking my death in the desert then beginning life anew as Brad, an itinerant manicurist, in Shingle Rock, Idaho. Let's keep it a secret, okay?

Not even the sharpest grandmother out there works that way. As tempting as it is to open your flap and spill, the number one rule of thumb is NO, you absolutely Cannot-with-a-Capital-C. Tell. Anyone.

I do think I handled the sticky issue of paving over old habits and haunts with new. Hopefully a plan to relocate completely—since an attempt to do this within the same city you previously occupied, no matter how big, could be doomed at the outset—will help a lot with keeping your lips zipped.

Some other perils that may arise and bump us out of our happy little hidey-holes? If you're escaping a criminal act, the answer is obvious. Police in even relatively small cities have an alarming number of resources at the tips of their fingers with which to try and track you down. If you've given them sufficient motivation, the other thing you can guarantee is they won't ever stop.

Violent crime, of course, will be top-lined. A murder file might get back-burnered after a year or two, but it really goes without saying (I hope!) that some enterprising detective with a hole in his or her caseload will one day pick that puppy back up again. The folks at the senior center tuning into CBS aren't the only ones who can get invested in a *Cold Case*.

In fact, if you're a (suspected, alleged, whatever other qualifier you care to add to make yourself feel better) murderer or any kind of violent criminal—especially a chronic violent criminal—then I probably should have said this at the outset: I'm not sure how much help this book will be to you. Of people who have targets on their backs, you will always be wearing the brightest, biggest, neon sign of a target. Simple measures for the average alleged embezzler or drug trafficker will not necessarily apply for you, my unfortunate friend.

For those accused of lower-echelon misdeeds that still might garner some prison time, now we're in the ballpark. For many of you, some of the heat might subside and stay at a simmer.

With noncriminals: Good Samaritans who ran afoul of gangs, dealers, killers, stalkers—the motivation of whoever is after you is just up in the air. In a way, it's in your best interest to sift through your plans and make sure they seem ironclad, so you're prepared to expect the unexpected. There's no good way to gauge how financially and emotionally invested any given private citizen might be in tracking you down. Best to stay light on your toes!

That in mind, I've assembled a list of simple principles. Write these down and refer to them daily. Hourly, even. Take them with you wherever you go. Sticking with these basic methods of operation could ensure you minimize those worrisome chinks in the armor you wrap around your plan to stay ghosted forever.

Don't speak. Simply: shut up. Don't say a word. Imagine for a moment that I'm your attorney and every single person you meet is a cop. Do me a favor and keep quiet. You have a right to remain silent about this and everything else, because anything you say can and will be used against you—and not just in a court of law.

No doubt. There are certain pursuits in life where doubt, even momentary and passing, can be a killer. They include but are not limited to: deadly hand-to-hand combat, walking on hot coals, and practicing the law. Also the act of removing yourself from your former existence and beginning a new one. If you don't have that level of confidence in what you're doing, either start looking for alternative solutions to your problems (if you're a criminal, a great attorney; if you're potentially in danger from a criminal, police protection—and a great attorney never hurts, either) or do as Alfred Hitchcock once instructed Ingrid Bergman to do when acting a scene she found unusually challenging: "Fake it, Ingrid." Fake it till you make it out alive.

Write it out. Be extra careful with this, but do it. Careful in that once you are certain you no longer need the written version, delete, burn, totally obliterate that damned thing. Take it with you when you go, then set it on fire and dump the ashes down the sewer.

But write it out. Use a spreadsheet if you have to. List each step of the plan, then each substep. Make notes on the side where you need to. Put approximate dates, give yourself a time line to get it done. Lawyers, authors, doctors—the list of professions that function best when there's some kind of plan down on paper goes on longer than the guitar solo in "Hotel California." If you've got that requisite lack of doubt and are feeling good about your road map along this journey, write it down. Give yourself checklists along the way, too. You'll feel that warm and fuzzy feeling of accomplishment each time you check something off.

Then, again: destroy all of it. The last thing in the world you want to leave behind is a step-by-step, bread-crumb trail leading directly to the mat on your doorstep that spells out the word "premeditated" in glow-in-the-dark letters.

Commit to the bit. Comedians use this phrase when talking about selling any part of an act. An audience can smell it when a performer has lost confidence in what they're doing, and will react accordingly. Hell, that's not just for comedy—it's true in the court of law, too. To stand in front of a judge or jury and attempt to defend anyone with any less than 110 percent conviction is the only way to guarantee, well, a conviction. Or lack of one, if you're on the side of the defense. Even if a client turned to me seconds before my closing argument and said, "Hey, buddy, I totally did stomp on all those baby kittens before I set those schoolchildren on fire," I can guarantee that no one in that jury box would see it on my face.

In your new life, this thing for which you've carefully planned and laid a lot of groundwork, you have to sell it, baby.

If that seems intimidating, double back to a point I've made on several occasions already: lay low. The less often you interact with other humans, the less acting you'll need to do. If you suffer from stage fright, a guiding principal of your new life is going to have to be "don't make waves."

Remember Joey Newts? That guy was an eccentric, sure, but on the whole the dude managed more than two full decades of laying low, doing his thing, and staying a mystery long after his death. One way Joey Newts managed was by not doing squat. He worked whatever jobs he could get that fit his skill set and didn't dig too deep into his background, lived in a low-key apartment, and didn't get too close to anyone. He kept his audience, so to speak, pretty small.

Clark Rockefeller? He was fine until his emotions shoved him onto a much bigger stage than his stories were prepared for.

Commit to the bit, yes. One hundred percent. At the same time, always play it to a chamber theater crowd. No big houses. That's part of how this life works. Try to steer clear of the spotlight, or you might find yourself lit by a helicopter's searchlight.

O.P.P. (Other People Problems)

Every element of this big show, this charade we're talking about putting into play, could bear volumes of discussion and finely detailed notes, but hey—even at my leisure, my time is at a premium. Just be glad I no longer charge in six-minute increments.

I wouldn't be providing you with adequate counsel in talking about potential pitfalls in the disappearance game if I didn't bite the bullet and deal with the one thing we've been talking about avoiding at all costs. What if you sense that you are under surveillance?

Someone could be on your tail for any number of reasons, not all of them related to trying to figure out if you are the you that you used to be (take a quick mental break and say that last bit five times fast; I'll wait).

To begin with: yes, hell is other people. An average schmoe or schmoette on their way home after a long day at work could end up followed on the road for a variety of frequently terrible reasons. Anyone who's ever stood on the subway knows that.

I always feel like . . . somebody's watchin' me. Seriously, how would you know if you're being followed? There's a little bit of bad news about that: often, if the follower is a professional, you won't. How good the tail is also depends on who you are and why someone thinks you're worth following in the first place.

If you're an international fugitive, I feel safe assuming there will be way more than one lone agent eyeballing you from behind an out-of-place copy of *Cat Fancy*. And it won't be your typical Keystone Kop, either. These investigators will be coordinated and careful and there's not a chance in hell that you'll see them coming.

When the stakes are lower, the most you'll have to deal with are a couple of cops, maybe a private detective, or a skip tracer (a slightly more corporate private dick, often sent out if your vanishing was connected to a wee tablespoon of embezzlement) then their surveillance techniques may be a little easier to spot.

Lights on, everybody home. There's no need to give up the small pleasures in life once you've adopted a new name and trajectory. Having said that, when you're out in public, first and foremost: never let your guard down. I don't care if it's St. Patrick's Day or Kwanzaa or F. Murray Abraham's birthday, you keep that pint glass full of ice water when you're out about town. Do what you will in the privacy of your new home, but when you're in public, remember that "in vino veritas," and those wine-truths could come back to bite you in the verit-ass.

And what's the thing that pilots say? Eight hours

bottle to throttle. Well, in your full-throttle new life, you're probably never going to have a guaranteed eight hours without worry. If you've managed to nail down a job or have any kind of regular public travel to do in your assumed guise, then it's alertness level orange at all times—and not even a sip of that sweet nectar of the gods to cloud your clear vision.

The trick to becoming Jason Bourne. This won't make you a master operator like the storied assassin, with wicked hand-to-hand combat skills or total command over every form of weaponry that falls in your hands, but it will give you a lead on just about every other person walking down the street. The trick is called "situational awareness," and we'd all be happier if more people practiced it.

On a basic level it's pulling your head out of your ass or your phone or whatever clouds are hovering nearby, and taking stock of your surroundings when you're in a public setting. The average man or woman marching down the street with their head bowed over a phone is at near zero situational awareness.

If you're out during the day, you can start practicing this in a simple way. Wear shades so that your eyes are difficult to track (that's one big reason so many feds seem to fetishize sunglasses, by the way) and make a point to size up as many people around you as you can.

Watch gestures, mannerisms, their eyes. Is that guy over there tracking you with his eyes? Is he doing it because he fancies your scarf, or because he's trying to see if you match a description on a BOLO or a missing persons flyer?

Don't just mark the people around you—mark the cars, too. Has that Chevy circled the block one more time than you'd reasonably expect it would take to find parking? Check the street you live on (and any adjacent ones), making note of cars that seem like they're parked at odd times, when others are gone. Or cars parked along whatever routes you use that are just idling, with a lone passenger inside. Sure, the driver could be finishing a sandwich before moving along with his or her own errands, but that doesn't preclude the idea that they could be keeping tabs on you, too.

In a way, focusing on observation like this can actually help alleviate the paranoia that comes with this whole thing, too. It's remarkable just how often no one is paying attention to anyone else at all. Try not to be offended that you're not the center of the universe, and appreciate it.

Avoid telegraphing your paranoia. So much easier said than done, huh? If this is a skill you may have developed a little late in life, it's no cakewalk to disguise that you are scoping out every single thing that's happening around you. Those shifty eyes will mark you as a mischievous shoplifter at best, and a demented sexual deviant at worst. "Subtlety" has to be your watchword, my friend.

Slow and steady keeps you free. If you are the hard-charging type who likes to keep up a fifteen-minute mile on a casual stroll, then this will be tough for you. Give up your East Coast big city stride, and dial it back to an unhurried Southern promenade.

In short: slow down. Leisurely paced chases are tricky to conduct, but they're ripe for experimentation. If you quicken your speed for a block or two, then suddenly drop down to a snail's pace: did someone nearby match you in lockstep? That person may be angling for an unpleasant rendezvous at a moment of their choosing—which is definitely not a recommended part of this program.

Unfortunately, if you spot a tail, certain options open to most people will not be available to you. Unless you are utterly convinced that your new identity is 100 percent ironclad, calling 911 in this situation is a bad idea (however: if you're just researching this stuff for grins and giggles and have no plans to change your identity, call 911 as soon as humanly possible if you have reason to believe you're being followed). It will just bring unwanted questions and curiosity from some of the last people you want poking at your story. So if John Q. Lawman is not at your disposal: what can you do?

Join the crowd. It's not a bad idea to get yourself to where the people are and stay there as long as possible. Any public venue where you're unlikely to get rousted, booted, whatever for walking in and taking a seat, use it. You might have to scrounge up a few bucks to buy a cup of coffee or ticket to the matinee (or whatever gains you entry to the space of your choice without scrutinization), but it'll be worth it. One advantage to this is it may give you a chance to turn the tables slightly, grab a vantage point from which you can get an eye on the person you believe is watching you. You may not have had time to do a proper once-over of your new shadow when the alarm bells went off in your head, so this will give you time to take a beat and evaluate.

Time for a cool change. When laying low and humming along in your new life, it's a good idea to stick with a steady, low-key pattern of behavior. A daily grind that's uncomplicated, as simple as you can make it. The possibility that someone is on your tail and trying to learn more about you flips that concept on its head. If you believe some paid detective or operative of any kind is tailing you, it's time to really throw a wrench into the cogs of your daily machinery and get unpredictable.

Tell you what I'd do. Let's say that my Monday-to-Friday work schedule has me clocking in 9:30 AM to 4:30 PM every day. I'm in my car by nine; I'm back at home by a quarter past five. The only stops I make are to fill up the car with gas or grab a few groceries.

Anyway, if one day I spy with sunglasses-shaded eyes a vehicle cruising just out of tailgating range that has been maintaining my speed no matter if I slow down or hit the gas, I'd get off at the next available exit, regardless of where it was. If my new pal followed, I'd get right back on the highway, keeping a careful eye on them.

If I didn't have any hard evidence that the surveillance was more than just something I was sensing (you know, that *feeling* you can get, the hair rising on the back of your neck), then I would shift my leave time back a half hour one day, fifteen minutes the next. I'd make part of the commute to work a walk. If I was taking the bus, I'd switch up which stops I used, and I'd leave early enough to factor that extra time into my schedule. Coming home, I might juggle my routine: randomly stopping for dinner or a movie—doing what looks like relaxed puttering, but it's puttering with serious purpose. Throw enough kinks in that routine you've established, you'll soon spot anyone making it a point to be where you are. People are creatures of habit—it's unnatural to suddenly switch up which grocery store you get your tomatoes from, so if you notice the same sweet grandmother that's always squeezing grapefruits at your local food emporium buying avocados at the store across town, she's probably not there looking for fruit.

Surveillance can take many forms. It can go on for quite some time, too. It depends on the one doing the surveilling and why. It isn't unheard of for law enforcement to keep one subject under watchful eyeballs for months at a time. If you begin to suspect this is going on, then it's time for you to make a change. Every day will need to be different. This will give you time to plan yet another exit strategy.

We've still got more to talk about before you go, of course. I've mentioned here and there that an important element of setting up your new life is the cover story. It's got to be plausible and easy to stick with. Essentially, you have to become a better-than-average liar. I wouldn't be doing my duty if I didn't give some examples of cover stories. A few as you segue into another life, and maybe a few more to tell once you're there—because for most of us, it's ultimately going to be impossible to avoid all social interaction.

In fact, that kind of avoidance can produce the exact opposite of what we want: attention. In our situation, it's not sexy to get a reputation for being "mysterious." That automatically invites unwanted questions. It doesn't bruise my ego at this stage of my life for a coworker to think I'm some boring old guy who spends his Sundays at the Farmers' Market. It means the heat will stay off, and I can chill out.

Cover Stories and Other Fictions

So you've made the decision that it's time to start laying down the tracks that will redirect this speeding train of life. Switches will be thrown, rails shifted, and suddenly—*screech*—you're off on a new track to parts unknown.

Sure, there's the old cold-turkey approach: just vanish. If it's very important to you that the folks who want to do you harm think you're a goner, then absolutely vanish overnight and forget about leaving any mystery behind.

The well-placed cover story that sets up an exit is worth considering, especially if you are simply bugging out of a situation that's become toxic over time, but that does not present an escalating form of danger. It buys you some time to sweep away the footprints marking the trail you're actually venturing out on.

Take Teddi, whose name has been changed to protect the innocent . . .

Teddi Gets Out

Teddi is thirty-five and married to Rex. Rex is what we like to call in the business—any business—an asshole. Rex works in medicine and has access to all the miraculous wonder-drugs the medical field has to offer. Teddi works hard. She has a higher-paying job than Rex, puts in a solid forty as a health-care administrator. Rex works nights so she's often alone and that suits her, because Rex is paranoid, his moods change on a dime, he's volatile. While they bonded over the wild world of pharmaceuticals originally, that very subject is now driving them apart.

One day, Teddi sees that a massive hospital is being built in Astana, the bustling capital of that hopping former Soviet satellite, Kazakhstan. She learns, to her delight, that the Kazakhs are keen to have American medical know-how.

Teddi surprises herself by coming up with a plan. She starts asking colleagues about Doctors Without Borders, and about medical field opportunities in other countries. She starts studying up on different languages, sees what sticks. She keeps up on current events and dives deep into world history. She memorizes maps and starts obsessively checking flight schedules of major airports near and far. She would crush Geography Jeopardy! if that were a thing.

One night when Rex is off work and seems more reasonably lucid than usual, she lays it out for him: her facility is losing money and she'll have to search for new employment soon.

She goes on to explain that there might be foreign opportunities for someone with her skill set—opportunities that pay very well.

At this point, Teddi's plan is indistinguishable from any other caring and responsible spouse's effort to salvage home and hearth. We should all be so lucky as to find a Teddi someday, right? And from the moment Rex grumbles his agreement with the plan, she's outwardly planning just as one would.

She studies Russian. She prepares to get her job and get out. She actually does so.

The foreign contract pays well, and Teddi starts socking away a nice chunk of each check. It's reserved for taxes, she says.

Eventually, Teddi discovers her work visa is up and maybe her job is, too—but that money is still socked away. Her passport is still good. She's befriended a Russian guy who is in tight with Putin's regime, which means this dude has the hookup.

So Teddi turns tourist. She doesn't ever bother booking that trip home. And then one day, she disappears.

This all takes some time, of course. Nothing is overnight. But Russia is a huge country and there is some dark and troubling stuff afoot there at any given time. It's also the kind of place where a rich guy can pull a few strings. Soon, Teddi has a new Russian name and a birth certificate certifying she was born in St. Petersburg.

Meanwhile, Rex is tipping some Adderall into an Altoids tin when his newest girlfriend comes up behind him and says, "Freeze—DEA."

He's never sure where the tip about his shenanigans came from, but he has a good idea. Not that there will be much to do about it from prison, with the tipster three thousand miles and an ocean away, living as a Russian citizen with a peculiarly American-sounding accent.

So maybe a few rules were broken with Teddi's tale, but she did some of the important things we've talked about: she developed a plan that fed her need for funds, came up with a very plausible reason to get the hell away, and lulled her abuser into thinking she was taking care of him in the bargain. Then once she was overseas and had a chance to start building her own life, she did so. Teddi did manage to cross the ocean and hold a job under her own name when she got there. She was also in a part of the world where changing times might make her goal of becoming a different person much easier than if she'd landed in a nation built with more bureaucratic bullshit.

If trying to take on a new identity in another country isn't your cup of tea, let's bring it back home and talk about Ron. This is the story of a guy much more like you or me.

Ron on the Run

Ron is the numero uno car salesman across the whole chain of dealerships in the Rust Belt. Everyone thinks he could easily manage his own flagship lot, be the big guy who sits at the fancy cocobolo desk at the back of the showroom, in full control of all the transactions around him. But that's not Ron. Our guy loves the seduction of gently soft-shoeing you into the loving embrace of a beautiful new Lincoln Town Car!

Ron's even been featured on flashy commercials for the dealership; the public loves him for his bright smile and colorful suits.

Ron has a problem, though. Even though he makes some pretty sweet money moving Cadillacs, Lincolns, and the like, he could always use more. So Ron does side work moving other automobiles that aren't exactly shipped direct from the factory. With these side transactions, he makes a good deal more and it's cold, hard cash that goes right into a bank account listed under his LLC (Limited Liability Company, a fairly easily established legal entity that can be used to open accounts and do business itself), which has been established under a name that wouldn't quickly be linked to him.

Ron's built up one hell of a nest egg!

One day Ron feels like a transaction with a new customer is a little, well, off. He can't really put his finger on why, but his antenna goes up. Maybe it was the guy's nice shoes, or maybe it was the way the dude called him "sir." Whatever it was, Ron begins to suspect that his unorthodox side business and tax-free kitty may have drawn attention from the wrong people. Whether it's the local cops, the feds or another outfit that fences stolen cars, he doesn't really know.

Ron just knows that he can feel little beads of sweat rolling down his talcum-powdered thighs.

A few years ago, Ron's younger brother Todd passed away. Don't worry, Ron's not some murderer; it was from natural causes. Ron was made executor of his estate. The whole memorial and cremation ceremony was very low-key and tasteful.

Ron had Todd taken to a funeral home run by a former love of Ron's, Annie. He knew Annie would handle his brother's remains in an honorable way. He also had a very special request. Knowing it's usually the responsibility of the funeral director to report deaths to the Social Security Administration, Ron asked Annie if she could misplace the paperwork on that for a few months, maybe even a few years.

Annie, as responsible as she was kind, balked a bit at this. "It's like this," said Ron, "Our poor old mom relied on Todd's disability payments"—from an injury, not cognitive or emotional disability—"and it sure would be nice if she could keep getting those for a while. Just until I've managed to save a little more to help her myself."

Annie couldn't resist good old smilin' Ron's charm and guess what? Todd's death was never reported to the social security folks.

That left Ron with some interesting advantages. First of all, his mother truly was helped by her younger son's government money, before she passed away herself. Secondly, Ron had access to the birth certificate, social security number, and various other information for someone who was not only just eighteen months younger, but also had the same last name as him.

At the time, Ron put Todd's IDs in a lockbox, as he did with most important documents (not to mention the generous profits from his side business). He had a feeling it all might be useful later. He also—very wisely—maintained a companionable relationship with Annie. Just to make sure everything was smooth.

Returning to Ron's hinky feeling after one of his off-the-books transactions—our man on the car lot begins to notice lookie-loos chatting up other sales folks. These inquisitive customers are reminiscent of the guy who called him "sir."

Hell, thinks Ron, there's something. And these lookie-loos: they test-drive, they sit and chat, but none of them ever buy. It's the end of the month! The deals don't get better than this, and still they're not biting?!

There must be shenanigans afoot.

Here's what Ron does: after investigating the Social Security Death Index (it's not hard to do, especially if you have access to certain genealogy databases) and noting that his brother doesn't show up as deceased, Ron has a heart-to-heart with himself.

He and Todd were about the same height, with different colored hair. They were the sort of siblings who could almost be mistaken for twins, if you weren't wearing the right glasses.

Ron heaves a big sigh and decides he'll give it a shot. He'll resurrect Todd.

Back in the city, Ron pockets his late brother's social security card. He grabs his birth certificate. He heads to his mom's place, which he owns and rents out now dear old ma has also passed away. Ron picks up an old tax notice from the state with Todd's name on it—a smallish debt his brother had left still comes up each spring, because as we've seen, the unfortunate Todd's death hasn't ever been recorded.

Now Ron has the three things he needs to establish a legitimate state-issued ID in Todd's name (but in Ron's image): birth certificate, official bill of some kind, social security card.

Ron does just that.

Over the next few weeks, he makes several other moves. He puts his mom's house on the market, knowing it will sell pretty quick (it does). He cashes out the sale and shifts that money into his LLC account.

Two states away, via an agent, he purchases a small, modest home under Todd's name. He sets up all the utilities in the same way. None of these transactions are connected to Ron's name at all. His commercials never get airtime south of Toledo, so he feels pretty comfortable that he won't be recognized as his charming salesman self.

Most importantly, Ron starts laying down a few lines to the good people at the car dealership. He puts some cover story gambits into play. They're vague, but still pointed. He mentions to an accounting clerk that he's worried about an out-of-town relative struggling with cancer. To a mechanic in the service bay, he admits that he's got some worrisome debts keeping him up at night.

Ron tells these stories and keeps them consistent. He's well aware that there's nothing like a good smokescreen to confuse anyone who might be trying to track you down should you decide it's time to head for the hills.

Then: he puts his plan into motion.

He cuts the outside lines going into his own house. He watches carefully to see if that brings any action on the street; it does not. His home isn't under surveillance yet, at least not at night.

Ron kicks in his own back door and begins trashing the place. It's not fun, he hates breaking his precious stuff, but what can you do? He even ends up leaving some blood drops he knows will be traced back to him. Injuries acquired during the struggle, of course.

After putting the finishing touches on the violent tableaux, Ron slips across several backyards quietly. There's a packed go-bag in a beat-up Honda parked a few streets away, a vehicle registered to Todd. Ron revs the engine, and just like that: he's gone.

Once he's settled down as Todd in his new town, he uses the nest egg he's brought along to give himself time to find a legit job, because new people in the neighborhood with no apparent means of support could invite suspicion.

Ron goes into retail, yes. But he sure as hell is no longer selling cars, and he's no local television star.

Ron, whose story may just be a little more real than Teddi's, is an example of a guy who both had some peculiar advantages—Annie the funeral director, a dead brother whose death was not well-reported, and a lack of extended family looking to chase him down—not to mention a sizable nest egg with which to begin his new life. His job in sales taught him to think in terms of social engineering. Even the most honest car salesperson you know has, at some point in their career, gone to bat with a bold-faced humdinger of a lie to close a deal for one reason or another, and they've done it with a straight face. I'd bet my new life on it.

Where Ron's story gets iffy is the prospect that the cops were definitely doing the chasing and not some illicit outfit pissed because he was horning in on their own business fencing stolen autos. Criminals wouldn't be so bad, but if the cops were after him, the dead brother move might screw Ron over big time. All it takes is one inspector to check his family history, see Todd's name, and have a lightbulb go off. Then Ron/Todd wakes one morning to the sound of a jackbooted cadre of the government's finest battering his front door into splinters.

Still, he had the official papers, the go-bag, and a very expertly rendered set of stories that might just leave everyone wanting to know his fate kind of confused as to where to start the manhunt.

Ron's a pretty good example of things going just about right. But what if they don't?

Leo's Last Ride

Leo is a good dude, but he's had some troubles. Early in life, Leo understood that he could make extra money as a "subcontractor," working some deals on the street on behalf of some powerful dudes.

He establishes a clientele pretty quickly. He's not a big operator, not the main moneyman—but Leo feels like he's just a small-time merchant with a conscience. Our buddy even has the good grace to turn away anyone who strikes him as too young!

Anyway, one day the most banal thing pushes him

off his chosen corner: construction. Cops directing traffic, torn-up pavement and sidewalk—if you've ever spent time in a city, you know the drill.

Leo picks the wrong corner to resume business. In alarmingly short order, our pal is on the shitlist of the biggest distributor in the city. Fearing retribution, Leo's own supplier skedaddles.

Leo has a few regulars, but his supplies dwindle—and worse, the big guy he pissed off isn't interested in a new agent; he's interested in demonstrating what happens when you step out of your own row and do business on the top man's block.

Leo is marked.

He comes up with a plan. First, he buys a fake ID from a buddy, Jared, and for good measure Jared throws in a birth certificate to go with it. Some dead dude, Jared says. Leo doesn't try to get a license.

He buys himself a scooter—a sedate silver number, cruising at thirty-five mph tops. He's sure it will get him where he needs to go.

He tells his mom that he's decided to join the army. She's shocked, but at the same time pretty pleased; he needed to get a new life, something better, and maybe the army will pay for his schooling. She always thought he'd make a fabulous actuary!

Leo's plan is pretty simple. Get to the highway on

the outskirts of the city, then ditch the scooter and jump aboard a late-running Greyhound bus—a ticket purchased in his name. He takes with him a good chunk of money, a lightly packed go-bag, and a smart phone he purchased still in the box from Jared.

Leo is never seen again. And not in the good way—the "sleep with the fishes" way.

I feel bad just thinking about good ol' Leo, but if you've been paying attention, you already know every misguided decision that led to his untimely demise.

Casually purchased fake papers from an acquaintance. If you're going to clue someone in to your new identity, make sure that you don't know them at all, or that they're someone you can trust when the sugar strikes the saucepan. What if Jared worked for that kingpin who had a bee in his bonnet? Jared's loyalty might not have measured further than a quick payout, or more likely—a grisly beating.

Came up with a lie for his mom that would've been very easy to spot. The military, you know, they're really good at keeping records of things. They're pretty militant about it, in fact.

Bought a ticket in his own name. What was the point of scooting his rear out of town if he was going to purchase a ticket linked directly to his old name? And if it was purchased in advance, it's a safe bet that it wasn't paid for with untraceable cash.

Didn't really think about all the supplies he had. If you had your antenna up at the end there, maybe you spotted one truly huge vulnerability for our unfortunate young friend: that smart phone. Whether the phone had a tracking app planted on it by our ID provider (et tu, Jared?) or Leo just happened to use it to chat with his mom some homesick evening later down the line, that phone is a ticking time bomb ready to blow up your new life.

The keyword is "wariness." There's preparation, yes— attention to detail while setting up some kind of exit strategy. After that, though, is when we stay wary.

Cover stories, smokescreens of fake information, are just as much for the folks who have transitioned into new names and personas as they are for folks like Ron, with his vague fears confusing all his coworkers.

Once you have established a new persona, new papers, new residence, the cold, hard fact of life is you will never be able to completely avoid human interaction. Even the full-on "hermit in the woods" approach isn't foolproof.

That's why the post-switch cover story is even more meaningful than the pre-absconding tale.

I'm not going to dictate case studies on this one because when it comes to the cover story you bring to the table after you've left everything else behind, it's a thing you'll need to tailor to your situation.

That means that this tissue of lies should follow a few principles, but it has to be shaped to who you are, your abilities, your appearance, et cetera.

You Self-Supporting So & So

A real spy has help in developing and supporting their cover story.

Let's assume then that the document-support part of the festivities, one of the many things a spy agency would handle for a covert operative, is something you've already taken care of.

Now what?

Appearance. This again, I know! Depending on your natural mien, it might be surprising how little you have to adjust to look like a different person. Ask yourself what your most prominent features are, and find ways to de-emphasize those. Red hair? Shave it or get regular dye jobs, regardless of gender. Only 2 percent of the Earth's population has red hair, so you guys tend to stand out. If you wore glasses, try to get contacts—or at the very least, switch to a totally different style. You might look sharp in some cat-eye frames!

Whatever you do to change your appearance, it needs to be something that's not too hard to maintain. New facial hair for men, new hairstyle for women—and if you were a habitually snappy dresser, try dialing it way down. Expand your wardrobe; maybe get a little more bohemian.

In a sense this is all about perfecting your performance. If you've come this far, you know you've got to commit to the bit. When it comes to altering your appearance as part of your new life reboot, keep that commitment front and center in your mind. Even if you haven't cut your hair since you were nine years old and it's currently tickling the back of your knees—grab some scissors and chop it into a short and sassy bob.

Or, say you're a guy who's always looked in the mirror and thought, "Man, I'm really not a mustache kind of guy." Step all over that self-conscious voice, buddy, and grow that flavor-savor out to '70s porn star proportions. That's the kind of commitment I'm talking about. This game doesn't stop with the 'stache, though.

Stick to your script. This isn't a repeat of the whole bit commitment thing, no. A new life requires a new set of background facts. This is your script.

I'm going to go with the simple brass tacks first.

Memorize the following: new birthday, street address, job, and whatever education or training you needed to do said job, your age (which can be different from your real age by a few years in either direction depending on the info you co-opted), and your fictional past family details.

Pretty simple stuff there, might take a few days of repetition to get it down. Then go further. Commit your new social security card to memory. I know my own and the one I use now and I'm proud to say that I haven't mixed them up yet.

Deeper details, more personal, even beyond numbers and dates—they are vital to making your story stick, to not ringing any suspicious bells. First date? First job? Location of your spring break trip senior year of college? The new you is a living, breathing individual with all sorts of memories and preferences that won't necessarily sync up with your old ones.

You liked that sad, pale beer in the past? Become a fan of the dark lagers, and have a couple that are in your top ten list to pull out when any Stein Snob starts interrogating you across the dinner table. You went to prom with a boy named Sue? Nope, now you went with a fish called Wanda, and the two of you had a grand old time gliding around the dance floor.

Be a spy like them. I'm talking about what actual

covert agents have to do when moving under the radar in a hostile nation. Blend in. Know the language—be fluent in your sleep, if possible. And if you're keeping it domestic, the "language" here will be more of a general familiarity with the local flavor.

If you've moved from Southern California, for example, to Down East Maine—that might as well be relocation to Scotland. The accent is radically different, so are the speech patterns. The *slang* is different. If any New Englander asks if you want "a mess of jimmies on your frappe," are you going to gasp with disgust or say, "Absolutely, that sounds wicked delicious?"

Answers to questions like that seem petty right now, but once you've begun moving along in your new groove, they slowly become very important, because isn't all of this about finding and embracing our inner chameleons?

Tell the lies you know. This requires a little unraveling: even though I'm encouraging you to become unusually gifted at deception, blending in, and various other spy-like stuff, I also have to admit that it's unwise to throw out everything you know.

As they say: the best lies contain a grain of truth.

So in manufacturing a new persona and whatever history you might need to go along with it, don't ignore everything that ever happened to you before: just shift it slightly.

If the embedded lies that come with living like this make you squirm and feel like you've lost touch with yourself, this should help.

For instance—if you were born in the South, there's always a chance a little bit of your homegrown accent is still buried in the words you say. In your new life, don't even bother trying to deny you've ever lived in the South. That will stick out to anyone who hears it when you say "heel" and "hill" and they sound like the same word. But if you're from Alabama, maybe claim to be a Mississippian (iffin' you know enough about the history and geography of Mississippi to pass as a card-carrying member of the Hospitality State). Keep your story just a little left of center.

Look, if you were a pretty decent pick-up musician, a homegrown fiend on the acoustic guitar, the keyboard, or the slide whistle, don't steer clear of that stuff forever. If you were a world-renowned trumpeter, try taking up the oboe—you'll get all that musical catharsis without the fear of someone noting your skill and seeing your photo in an old copy of Brassy Illustrated.

Anytime it's possible to embed some truth in the things you say, it's going to add a layer of authenticity when interacting with others. It's up to you to pick and choose as you go, figure out what will work for you and not lead to a raised eyebrow or unwanted questions.

It's worth reminding you at this point, too: even if a ton of this is spy-like stuff, one of the things you want to avoid is giving the impression you may actually be a spy. Because what's the most natural reaction to that? Extreme interest at your expense.

Here we are again. We're not at an end, no, not even close to done, at least in spirit. This subject could fill an illicit library or two. There are plenty of resources online, and maybe even some other books out there that come at it from a slightly different angle. But buyer beware, especially of online libraries intended for survivalists and antigovernment types: many of their documents describing methods for dropping out of society's grasp were totally relevant right up to the year 2000 or so.

The Internet taking over every aspect of life the way it has put kind of a cramp in some of the old ways.

Recall our strange buddy Joey Newts, aka Joseph Newton Chandler III, aka the man who wasn't there, somehow. Back when he ordered the birth certificate of the dead, real Joey Newts, it was pretty easy to do.

It's just a different ball game now.

Afterword: The Long Con

I've been acting as a sort of counselor here, so you'll understand if the old Saul's instincts bubble up a lot. In the interest of full disclosure then, let me tell you: I've taught you a lot about slipping off the grid and running under that radar, but in good conscience I can't just wave my hand in benediction and tell you to go.

The professionals who assisted me and a lot of the research I did taught me one thing loud and clear above all else: this is a real gamble. Every single day, The Man gets better and better at organizing all the spinning spirals of zeroes and ones we fire across our keyboards and devices into full-color portraits of each and every one of us.

Bald-faced honesty time? Not sure how much longer anyone will be able to do this kind of thing without serious inside help. That's sad, too. It means there may come a day when those in danger from crime syndicates, stalkers, or cartels (who aren't deemed high-enough-profile witnesses) will just be at the mercy of circumstance. The government only has so many programs and agents it can use to babysit witness protection. That program may even shrink, even as the need for an ability to drop out of sight but still live your life as best as you can increases.

And if you've heard all the "buyer beware" warnings and advisories about the difficulty, there's something else you should know: jumpstarting a new life can be tough on the old ticker.

Not just your actual heart, but your emotions as well. Figure out what you're comfortable with before you commit to giving something like this a shot.

There are people who've tried to take a loved one, even families along. It's not easy. Think about the difficulties in two people sticking to one story.

James "Whitey" Bulger, the Boston mobster who ran the legendary Winter Hill Gang, went on the lam with his attractive, blonde lady friend and a lot of cash in hand. Bulger made it all the way across the country to Southern California. There he did exactly what people should do. He hunkered down. The man suspected of ordering and committing so many mob homicides put on a comfortable hat and strolled along the beach with his friend. They made no waves.

Bulger had money, he'd thoroughly cut all ties to his previous life, and to this day feds are convinced he had some help apart from his girlfriend. But in the end, after sixteen years, he was arrested. That's because a former Miss Iceland happened to live in his Santa Monica neighborhood and recognized him.

It's hard to not feel like it was always a matter of

time for Whitey. You know how it's tricky to recognize people out of context? Walking around with your known significant other is often just the kind of context that can switch on a lightbulb in the mind of a passerby.

That was a master criminal. Now imagine trying the same maneuver for any reason with a spouse and kids, or just kids. Can you trust your kids to stick to your lies? Could you expect them to? If so—what the heck kind of parent have you been?

But that's outside the scope of this discussion.

It seems like it's got to be a lonely enterprise, then. And dwelling on that can really drill deep into spongy, melancholy recesses of your mind.

If I have any recommendation, it's not that you stay some sad cenobite stuck in the dark all night long. I think a new life probably ought to mean actually living, you know? Make the change on your own. Get established. Very slowly and with thought, staying alert the whole time, start dropping a root here or there. It'll keep you from falling down when the wind starts to pick up.

Pause, take a look around you, see if anyone is watching. Speak when spoken to, but be very slow and measured about when you open up and start that conversation.

Look, call it what it is: it's a con job. It's the con of a lifetime, and the con is your new life.

To do it right you have to understand the art of the long con, which is something like living theater. It comes complete with costumes, lines, props, even background research to really dig into the deeper meaning of the whole thing—which is, in this case, just staying alive. You'll make 'em weep if you perform it right—and you've only got one chance at a captive audience, so never break character.

To get off the grid and keep on moving under your new name is not just running—it's a form of *winning*. I'm not trying to convert you to some kind of Cult of the Willing Disappearance, but I'm pretty convinced at this point that life might be a little more palatable if more people had this option available.

Now and then I think about what they used to call potter's fields. Those were cemeteries where cities would bury the unknown dead, who we'd call John or Jane Doe today, followed by a string of digits matching a coroner's file.

It's an image that makes you pretty sad, right? It's a graveyard in some lonely corner of the city, full of strangers to each other and everyone who encounters them now. I imagine plenty of people who said "screw this ridiculous clown show" to the life they were living and opted for a hobo existence are lying under a numbered metal cross in a Potter's Field.

Over time, I've stopped feeling too down about that. Sure, it's a gloomy image, the kind of thing that might give you a shiver . . . but what if some of those anonymous folks under that dirt weren't remotely the lost souls we all assume they were?

I think a few of them, maybe a pretty generous chunk, may have succeeded in doing exactly what they set out to do. I don't like to think about the fact that a cancer diagnosis made him conclude he was going out on his own terms, but a John Doe like Joey Newts—no one knows who he is today. He ended up a pile of remains in the middle of nowhere, and all we've got is a mystery.

In a sense, that dude succeeded maybe even beyond his wildest dreams, if his goal was to disappear from whatever he thought was chasing him.

This thing we're talking about doing, I don't think it's ever been an easy decision for anyone. Perhaps too often it's an act of quiet desperation, an effort to preserve a little more living and get a little extra juice out of life.

Say it goes exactly as you want it to. Years and years pass, and you're still rocking that name you pulled off a birth certificate intended for a completely different baby back in the day. Then something natural happens: heart attack, gentle stroke in your sleep, an unfortunate collision with a cement truck. The coroner pulls your prints, checks your dental records, maybe even runs your

DNA . . . but investigation determines no one can figure out who the hell you are anymore. However you did it: you got out, you changed your life, and when it came time to pay the piper or play foosball with Satan or whatever happens at the end, you remained a mystery.

In the end, that means you came out on top. Unless one of them was behind the wheel of that godforsaken cement truck, the bastards never got you. A long con done to perfection.

I call that a win. Now get going—get on with your life. And if it that journey up shit creek ever becomes too unmanageable, remember: you can buy a paddle.